THE ARCHAEOLOGY
OF THE
NEW TESTAMENT

"Truth shall spring out of the earth" (Ps. 85:11)

3.0

THE ARCHAEOLOGY
OF THE
NEW TESTAMENT

by

E. M. Blaiklock, Litt. D.
Emeritus Professor of Classics
University of Auckland
New Zealand

ZONDERVAN PUBLISHING HOUSE
GRAND RAPIDS   MICHIGAN

PREFACE

WHAT IS ARCHAEOLOGY? DEFINITION CAN BE TOO COM-
prehensive and become, in the process, description. For
example, when, at the beginning of this century, awareness
was growing of the complex nature of the subject, the *Century Dictionary* said: "Archaeology is that branch of knowledge which takes cognizance of past civilizations, and in-
vestigates their history in all fields, by means of the remains
of art, architecture, monuments, inscriptions, literature,
language, customs, and all other examples which have survived." R. A. S. Macalister, on the other hand, is too brief
and circumscribed in his definition: "Archaeology is the
branch of knowledge which has to do with the discovery
and classification of the common objects of life."

A brief but adequate definition might be:

"Archaeology is that branch of historical research which
draws its evidence from surviving material traces and remains of past human activity." Such a statement allows room
for the increasing scope of such investigation, as modern
techniques render significant hitherto neglected evidence.
From air-photography to Carbon 14 dating, the archaeologist
has multiplied and improved his tools and methods in a
hundred ways. Nor has the refinement of both theory and
practice reached the end of its development.

The extent to which such research has thrust back the
frontiers of historical knowledge is apparent in every sphere.
In New Zealand, the land where these words are written,
the whole picture of the Polynesian occupation of the area
has been transformed in the last ten years by the examination
of the fragile debris on the sites of the "moa-hunters'" camps.
Since Heinrich Schliemann's enthusiasm gave Troy and
Mycenae back to western knowledge a century ago, and
Arthur Evans, at the beginning of this century, revealed what
lay beneath the soil of Crete, a succession of archaeologists of
increasing skill and effectiveness have given back to history

the whole complex of Aegean and Central Mediterranean civilizations, which are not without reference to the archaeology of the lands of the Bible.

When Samuel Johnson remarked in his pontifical fashion, some two centuries ago, that "all that is really known of the ancient state of Britain is contained in a few pages, and we can know no more than the old writers have told us," he was representing the attitude of the day. To be sure, when he talked in the George Inn of Fleet Street, Roman London lay beneath his feet, with part of its surviving wall within five minutes walk of his house, up the narrow lane across the street. But the eighteenth century had not learned to read the record in the soil.

Johnson had not realized that man writes history unconsciously and indelibly in more ways than one. Man tells his story in the election slogan scratched on a Pompeian wall, in a scrap of potsherd marked with a candidate's name, in the redwood chips of a Pueblo cave, in the split moa bones of a New Zealand swamp, in the papyrus remnants from a Fayum rubbish heap, in the brown stain of Roman ditch and posthole in a London cellar, in gravestone and inscription, in coins lost and buried, in his own frail bones laid at last in Roman catacomb, Danish bog, or Saxon burial barge, in house foundations, and time-defying trench and earthwork. Man's footprints are inevitable and manifold and it is to the credit of the modern world that man has learned to trace, to recognize, and to read the story thus recorded.

In the somber age in which we live, research has been overshadowed by the scientist. For good and ill chemist and physicist have changed the pattern and prospects of human life. And humanity at large, dazzled by such achievement, has been unaware of vast increases in knowledge in less obvious but no less important regions of the mind.

Two events awakened the general public to the new science and the knowledge it was giving as recently as the early twenties. The first was Carter's discovery in 1922 of

Pharaoh Tutankhamen's tomb in the Valley of the Kings. Since then the newspapers, and particularly the *London Illustrated News,* have realized that intelligent readers find archaeology absorbing. The second event was the publication in 1924 of the earlier volumes of the Cambridge Ancient History, which revealed to a more select reading public the successes which archaeology had already achieved. This was, no doubt, the moment Sir Mortimer Wheeler had in mind when he spoke of archaeology being discovered "not only by the public but by the professors."

The literary record, at any rate, is now read side by side with the evidence which archaeology supplies, and more often than not with results in all spheres which rebuke the habitual scepticism of a century ago. It was the mood of the nineteenth century to question and distrust tradition. It has been the experience of the twentieth century that tradition, even when embedded in myth and legend, must be handled with care and circumspection.

In more than one sphere it has been shown that what the past said about itself was in the main more likely to contain truth than falsehood. Schliemann's discovery of Troy and Mycenae, and Sir Arthur Evans' work in Crete, the ancient home of the Philistines, provided classical scholars with chastening illustrations of this fact.[1] The decipherment in 1953 of the Linear B Script has been an exciting and revealing epilogue to this story.

Striking vindications of biblical historiography have taught historians to respect the authority of both Old Testament and New, and to admire the accuracy, the deep concern for truth, and the inspired historical insight of the varied writers who gave the Bible its books of history. At first it was the Old Testament which came to vivid life. From Layard's discovery of Nineveh, over a century ago, which initiated the era of biblical archaeology, to the more recent

---

[1] Professor L. R. Palmer's researches suggest that Evans' conclusions will be heavily revised in their chronology.

near-tragedy of Wendel Phillips' attempt to excavate Sheba,[2] which revealed the exciting possibilities of new discovery, and the still more recent underwater archaeology on the Dead Sea, and the investigation of Masada, the story makes a fascinating record of exploration. Garstang's work at Jericho, Woolley's excavation of Ur, Starkey's discovery of the Lachish ostraka, the finding of the Tell-el-Amarna letters, the Ras-Shamra tablets, the stele of Hammurabi, the Moabite Stone, the Siloam Tunnel, these and a score of other astonishing events punctuate three generations of Old Testament archaeology, and offer promise of abundance yet to find.

The archaeology of the New Testament was later in the field. The following chapters will show some of its beginnings in the work of Grenfell, Hunt, and Ramsay at the close of the last century. Its discoveries do not contain the dramatic moments such as those Layard enjoyed when the sand fell away from the winged bulls of Nineveh, when Woolley found the headdress of the royal lady of Ur, or when Garstang first saw the stones of Jericho.

And yet drama does not need stage properties so vast or strange. It was surely a moment of high triumph for Hunt when he deciphered the word KARPHOS (a mote) on a scrap of papyrus, and knew that he held a sheet of the sayings of Christ almost contemporary with the writing of the gospels; or, indeed, for the Abbe Cumont, when he was first confronted with the stone slab from Nazareth.

Glance back at Macalister's definition of archaeology quoted above. "The discovery and classification of the common objects of life" goes far to cover its activities in the study of New Testament archaeology, which sometimes appears to have no other major task. Its stock in trade is discarded paper, the humble gravestone, the petty inscription. Its future work will have little to do with the ruins of city and palace, and the burial of kings; it will leave to others the more pretentious monuments of the ancient world,

---

[2] See *Qataban and Sheba,* published 1955.

and build its future story around such "common objects of life" as the Christian lamp, which the summer of 1956 saw found at Caerleon, the Christian grave relics of the York Museum, the chapel murals in the Lullingstone villa, or the fragment of the fourth gospel, found in 1935, which took back the manuscript tradition of that famously vindicated book to within a generation of its author. It will find a widening sphere in the closer investigation of the Catacombs; it will join hands with the Roman historian in the elucidation of life in the highly Christianized provinces of Asia and North Africa. Papyri, still unearthed or undeciphered, will no doubt have much to offer. The discovery of the famous Dead Sea Scrolls in 1948 shows what possibilities lie here.

THE PAPYRUS RYLANDS GRK. *457 is a fragment of John's gospel dating back to the first half of the second century* A.D.

The spade has obviously not yet finished with the Bible. "I believe in the spade," said Oliver Wendell Holmes. "It has fed the tribes of mankind. It has furnished them water, coal, iron, and gold. And now it is giving them truth — historic truth, the mines of which have never been opened till our time."

CONTENTS

ILLUSTRATIONS

THE PAPYRI OF EGYPT

CHAPTER 1

THE PAPYRI OF EGYPT

THE ARCHAEOLOGY OF THE NEW TESTAMENT HAS MUCH to do with waste paper, and before embarking on chapters which will speak of little else, it is well to devote a few pages to papyrology. Speaking to a learned Oxford audience in 1937, Sir Frederic Kenyon mentioned the surprising fact that the word "papyrology" was first used only in 1898, and somewhat apologetically, in a review of the second British Museum catalogue. The word "papyrus" was old enough. It goes back to Theophrastus in the fourth century before Christ, and its lineal descendant "paper" is a common enough word today.

Papyri — Ancient Convenience

It is difficult to imagine what life would be like without the commodity and convenience which the word signifies. In a moment of humor, a branch of self-expression in which he did not shine, Thomas Babington Macaulay wrote:

About four hundred years after the Deluge, King Gomer Chephoraod reigned in Babylon. He united all the character-

15

istics of an excellent sovereign. He made good laws, won
great battles, and white-washed long streets. He was, in consequence, idolized by his people, and panegyrized by many
poets and orators. A book was then a serious undertaking.
Neither paper nor any similar material had been invented.
Authors were therefore under the necessity of inscribing their
compositions on massive bricks. Some of these Babylonian
records are still preserved in European museums; but the
language in which they are written has never been deciphered.
Gomer Chephoraod was so popular that the clay of all the
plains round the Euphrates could scarcely furnish brick-kilns
enough for his eulogists. It is recorded in particular that
Pharonezzar, the Assyrian Pindar, published a bridge and four
walls in his praise.

Macaulay, needless to say, wrote his essay on the Royal
Society of Literature before the Babylonian script was deciphered, and his history and archaeology are quite sadly
awry. On his main point, however, there is little doubt. A
vast blessing was conferred on men by the unknown
Egyptian who invented ink, and found that the stem of a
river plant could be sliced into writing paper.

The plant which, in James Baikie's phrase,[1] "was destined
to be the instrument of so great a deliverance," was the
cyperus papyrus, a sedge which still grows plentifully in the
Sudan where it reaches the height of twenty-five feet. In
ancient days, as abundant evidence proves, the papyrus grew
also in the northern Nile valley, especially in the rich swamp-
lands of the Delta. Very early in Egyptian history it was
adopted as an emblem in Lower Egypt, to match the lotus
emblem of the upper division of the land. The papyrus is a
graceful plant and may be seen in pictures of Egyptian goddesses, held in the hand as symbol of divinity; its clustered
buds gave the architect a theme for decoration.

The papyrus stem had manifold uses. Bound in bundles,

---

[1] *Egyptian Papyri and Papyrus-Hunting*, p. 16. It is Baikie who recalls
Macaulay's little-known essay.

THE BUNDLES OF PAPYRUS, *carried by Bedouin women,*
are to be woven into mats.

for example, it provided handy rafts or canoes, for use in those bird-hunting expeditions in the fen-lands beloved of Egyptian sportsmen. But above all the tough pellicles of the stem gave mankind its first cheap and practicable writing material.

Pliny the Elder, the Roman admiral and scientist, has left a long description of the manufacture of writing material from the papyrus stem. It was cut into thin slices and the best pieces were of course the widest, from the middle diameter of the stem. This was called "hieratic paper" because it was devoted in earlier times only to the writing of books of religion. Placed crisscross on the board, the slices of reed were beaten together and pressed until the natural glue of the plant bound the sheets into a strong thin lattice of fiber.

According to Pliny, the Emperor Claudius, most scholarly

of the Roman rulers of the first century, took some interest in the quality of papyrus. Pliny writes: "The reason was that the thin paper of the period of Augustus was not strong enough to stand the friction of the pen, and moreover, as it let the writing show through, there was a fear of a smudge being caused by what was written on the back, and the great transparency of the paper had an unattractive look in other respects. Consequently the foundation was made of leaves of second quality and the woof or cross layer of leaves of the first quality. Claudius also increased the width of the sheet, making it a foot across. There were also eighteen-inch sheets called *macrocola,* but examination detected a defect in them, as tearing off a single strip damaged several pages. On this account Claudius' paper has come to be preferred to all other kinds."

The surface was smoothed with pumice and the result was a durable writing paper. If kept dry there is no limit to its survival. South of Cairo it never rains, and in fortunate consequence the writings of dwellers in Egypt under five empires — Egyptian, Persian, Greek, Roman and Islamic — have survived to charm, amuse, or instruct the modern world. It is a sad fact that papyrus rolls, when burned on a campfire, fill the desert night with a pleasant aroma, and that the Bedouin have earned the wrath of scholarship by burning countless rolls of literature for which most scholars would today exchange the Koran, and all else the Arabs have written.

Papyri — Wealth of Human Record

There are papyri in Egyptian, Hebrew, Greek, and Latin. There are literary papyri which have proved important contributions to the corpus of Aristotle, to Greek elegy, and Greek comedy. The non-literary papyri date from 311 B.C. to the seventh century. They come from the wrappings of mummies, the stuffed bodies of sacred crocodiles, and from mere 'wastepaper heaps, all manner of documents which have the same degree of unity one might find in the sacks of wastepaper sent to any paper mill for pulping.

They have proved, wrote J. H. Moulton[2] half a century ago, a treasure which has been perpetually fruitful in surprises. The attention of the classical world has been busy with the lost treaty of Aristotle and the new poets Bacchylides and Herodas, while theologians everywhere have eagerly discussed new Sayings of Jesus. But even these last must yield in importance to the spoil which has been gathered from the wills, official reports, private letters, petitions, accounts, and other trivial survivals from the rubbish heaps of antiquity.

The wonder is such a wealth of material remained for so long unnoticed. References to papyri go back to the middle of the eighteenth century, and are scattered through the sparse records of early nineteenth-century archaeology, but it was not until the last decade of the century that the unique value of the papyrus documents was recognized and systematic search and preservation begun. Professor B. R. Rees tells the story[3] in his inaugural lecture given at Cardiff in 1960. He writes:

Sir Flinders Petrie, excavating an ancient cemetery at Gurob in the Fayyûm in the winter of 1889-90, found a number of mummies enclosed in papyrus cartonnage; this cartonnage, when broken up was seen to be made of Greek documentary and literary texts of the third century B.C., the now famous Petrie Papyri, which include parts of the *Laches* and *Phaedo* of Plato written down within a hundred years of his death, some more Homer, and about a hundred lines of the lost *Antiope* of Euripides. About the same time the British Museum acquired through Sir Ernest Wallis Budge a parcel of papyrus rolls which was to create the greatest sensation yet. Already, even before the word itself was invented, there were two great names in papyrology — those of Ulrich Wilcken and Karl Wessely; a third was now to be added, that of Frederic Kenyon, for it was to him that the British Museum entrusted

2 *Grammar of New Testament Greek,* Vol. I, Prolegomena, p. 3.
3 University of Wales Press, 1960.

the task of finding out exactly what Budge's acquisitions were.

Professor Rees quotes Kenyon:

It was on the 30th of January, 1890 that I was first introduced to them. I well remember my first sight of them, laid out under glass on long tables. The hand-writings were for the most part totally unfamiliar. One, a small roll of poetry, looked easy to read, and so it was as far as mere decipherment went, but the matter was strange and often difficult, so it was reserved for further examination. The two longest were in small and (at that time) difficult hands; but it was possible to discern that one was historical and one medical, while a third, in not very dissimilar writing, was oratorical. The latter was immediately identified as Isocrates' *On the Peace* and the next day a letter of Demosthenes was recognized. The next discovery, after some days' steady transcription work, was Hyperides' *Against Philippides*. Presently the historical treatise was taken in hand. I remember that progress was slow at first, as the first column was a good deal damaged, but my suspicions as to its identity were aroused. I remembered having heard at Oxford, in a lecture by Dr. Macan, of the fragments of Aristotle's *Constitution of Athens* which had been identified at Berlin. I sent for Rose's edition of the fragments of Aristotle and kept my eye on it; and on 26th February I find it recorded that I had identified the papyrus as the lost Aristotle. Eleven months later the first edition was given to the world — very inadequately done, through hurry and inexperience, but at least providing much material for other scholars to work on.

The story is not yet finished. In 1956 the collection of the sayings of Christ known popularly as the *Gospel of Thomas*, was brought out of Egypt.[4] In 1959 a lost play of Menander from a recently discovered papyrus was produced in Geneva, and the famous Greek writer of comedies, without whom the Romans would not have had Plautus and Terence, marked up his final triumph by appearing in the Third Programme of the BBC. His newly discovered play, *Dyscolos* or *Grumpy Man*, was acted.

4 See p. 59.

The Papyrus Industry

Our gratitude then to the unknown discoverer of the use of the papyrus reed, and no less to the commercially-minded Greek rulers of Egypt who controlled the export of the manufactured material. Papyrus-farming was, in fact, big business in Egypt, and before turning to the New Testament aspects of the theme we may look at a lease for a papyrus marsh dating from 5 B.C., somewhere very near the date of the Nativity, which will be the theme of the next chapter. Observe, too, the legal thoroughness of that bureaucratic age:

To Protarchus from Dionysia daughter of Achilleus, of civic rank, with her guardian Eudemus son of . . . , and from Hierax son of Tithoes and Papus son of Andronicus, both Persians of the Epigoni. Concerning the matters that have been in debate we agree with each other on the following terms: Whereas Hierax and Papus have leased from Dionysia for three years from Thoth of the current 26th year of Caesar, the papyrus marsh belonging to her and her son, who is a minor, Achilleus son of Ptolemaeus, in the area of Arsinois, in the place called Colpus, which marsh was formerly owned by Hierax son of Hierax under its present boundaries, being bordered by the place called Batheia and that which bears the name of Dioecetus, and by Pisat and Emoui and for a certain distance by Telkaror, at a fixed yearly rent of 5000 drachmae of Ptolemaic silver free from deduction of any kind and clear of expenses, on the understanding that they shall pay this sum to Dionysia every year in monthly installments of 250 silver drachmae from Thoth to Mecheir and of 583 drachmae 2 obols from Phamenoth to Mesore; they shall therefore take up the lease on these terms for that period. It shall not be lawful for them to pay the workmen employed under the lease more than the current wages at Colpus, and they shall make a special payment every year of 1000 loads of papyrus with six bundles in each, and in working the property leased they shall . . . the suitable portions and treat the remainder with due consideration and not use pickaxes nor gather immature . . . nor cut from boats, nor work the property partially, nor sell articles made of rushes, nor sublet the land to others

nor pasture either their own or others' cattle in the marsh, and
whatever cattle they find there they shall remove at their own
cost, and they shall . . . the marsh at the proper times, and
the streams and the cross cuttings on their land they shall
fill in and excavate and reshape and render navigable, just as
they received them, at their own expense. And in the event of
. . . aggression or inundation or destruction of war, or if owing
to civic causes or through government . . . there is a stoppage,
or if any circumstances natural or supernatural affects the lease,
Dionysia shall have no responsibility and it shall not be lawful
for the lessees to abandon the lease within the period. If they
infringe any of these conditions, they shall straightway be
liable to arrest and be imprisoned until they . . . have paid to
Dionysia the amount which they owe for rent increased by one
half and for every load which they fail to deliver at the current
price and in addition a penalty of 1000 silver drachmae; and
it shall be lawful for Dionysia, if they break their contract, to
evict them within the period and lease the land to others and
exact the deficit as it stands at the date of re-letting, Dionysia
having the right to execution upon the lessees or any one of
them whom she chooses and upon all their property as if by
legal decision, all assurances produced by them and all resort
to protection being invalid. But if they fulfil the contract in
accordance with the conditions above stated, Dionysia shall
give them undisturbed possession of the lease for the period
and allow them to appropriate the fruits of it and not evict
them within the period nor exact any further payment, otherwise she shall herself forfeit the damages and costs and the like
penalty as if by legal decision, in addition to the agreement
remaining valid. The lessees shall deliver the 1000 loads at the
harbour of Anolmethius. We request (your sanction).

There are a few words of doubtful significance, but such
is the main purport. The closing words are addressed to the
head of a Control Board who had to sanction the lease. Big
business indeed, and oddly modern. . . . And today the
papyri are a major academic preoccupation with some of the
world's best scholarship devoted to their elucidation.

ARCHAEOLOGY AND THE NATIVITY

CHAPTER 2

ARCHAEOLOGY
AND THE NATIVITY

J. H. MOULTON, IN THE PASSAGE QUOTED IN THE PRECEDING chapter, spoke of "wills, official reports, private letters, petitions, accounts, and other trivial survivals from the rubbish heaps of antiquity." These "trivial survivals" have provided documents which throw vivid light on the birth of Christ, for among them are the enrollment forms which were used by William Mitchell Ramsay to establish the periodic nature of the Roman census, and underline the historic realities behind the magnificently told story in the third gospel.

The Assignment to Home Towns

A public notice provides a starting point. It has emerged from the rainless sand, with its first paragraph still clearly legible, and dated A.D. 104. It runs:

Gaius Vibius, chief prefect of Egypt. Because of the approaching census it is necessary for all those residing for any cause away from their own districts to prepare to return at once to their own governments, in order that they may complete the family administration of the enrolment, and that the

25

THE TOWN OF BETHLEHEM, *as viewed south to Manger Square and the Church of the Nativity. Terraced cultivation on the slopes are visible in the foreground.*

tilled lands may retain those belonging to them. Knowing that your city had need of provisions, I desire. . . .

At this point the document becomes too fragmentary to decipher. But such was the notice which a carpenter named Joseph found posted up in Nazareth one day, and read with a sinking heart. The Roman bureaucrats had little care for the comfort of those whom they ruled, and for census purposes it was convenient to gather the population in their own home towns.

It was probably legally necessary for both Joseph and Mary to present themselves, in accordance with the regulations, in Bethlehem. It was no doubt in conformity with a law mentioned twice in the closing chapters of the book of Numbers[1] that Mary had been betrothed to Joseph. Daughters, the law stated, who find themselves heirs to their father's property, must marry within the tribe. Thus Jesus, who was "the Son of Mary," of the royal line of David, could only be "King of the Jews" if He were reckoned as the legal

[1] Numbers 27:1-11; 36:1-13. (See J. N. Geldenhuys' *Commentary on the Gospel of Luke*, pp. 150-155.)

son of a member of the same tribe. Hence the genealogy of Joseph in Matthew's gospel. In Luke's gospel, Joseph is called "the son of Eli," and this must have been Mary's father, Joseph being considered the legal heir in the absence of sons. This, according to one theory,[2] is the explanation of the variant genealogies in the two gospels, and it is eminently reasonable.

It may, therefore, have been obligatory for the Holy Family to journey, at that precarious hour, to Bethlehem. Remembering the imperious Roman regulation, some have assumed the presence in the little town of sundry other personalities. Hillel, the great Pharisee, was, it appears, of David's royal line, and in spite of his great age, may have been there that day. And were his son Simeon, and his grandson Gamaliel, at whose feet Paul was to sit, also present? And did this considerable party fill the inn, leaving only the stable for the late arrivals, who had journeyed more tenderly and toilfully?

The Lodging in Bethlehem

It may, incidentally, be possible to identify the inn. Jeremiah (14:17) speaks of a certain "geruth," or "inn," which "is by Bethlehem." It was in the possession of one Chimham. Was this a descendant of Chimham, son of Barzillai, who, because of his father's beneficence to the exiled David (II Sam. 19:31-38), was treated by the king as a son? Did he become thus, as the son of a great sheep-rancher, the steward of the royal sheep-lands at Bethlehem? Did he build a hostelry which remained in the family after the stable fashion of the East, to provide a refuge in Jeremiah's day, and a rendezvous for shepherds (Luke 2:15) in New Testament times?

Pure speculation, no doubt, but there is one point in which legend and ancient art have presented us with a pic-

---

[2] For another suggestion see J. Gresham Machen, *The Virgin Birth of Christ*, pp. 203 sqq.

ture somewhat out of focus. The "lowly cattle shed" of the carol gives an incorrect impression. As a visitor of David's line, for all her poverty, Mary might naturally have expected the best accommodation, but the "kataluma," or "the guest-chamber," which should not be translated "inn," was already occupied. The host gave his next best accommodation, without thought of slighting his guest. It would probably be a rock-cut cavern with a raised platform, where visitors could sleep in sight of their tethered beasts and stacked luggage. They would not thus regard themselves as ill-treated.

The Census

The next morning Joseph had some documents to file with the authorities. From the Egyptian papyri come many examples of the statutory returns and declarations made by the subject of Rome in the periodic enrollments. The following are two interesting examples. The first dates from A.D. 48, and is a document of the fourth census after the one mentioned in the gospel of Luke:

To Dorion chief magistrate and to Didymus town clerk, from Thermoutharion, the daughter of Thoonis, with her guardian Apollonius the son of Sotades. The inhabitants of the house belonging to me in the South Lane are: Thermoutharion a freedwoman of the aforesaid Sotades, about 65 years of age, of medium height, with honey-colored complexion, having a long face and a scar on the right knee. . . . (A line is missing here which describes a second woman) . . . I, the aforesaid Thermoutharion (the document continues with an affidavit), with my guardian the said Apollonius, swear by Tiberius Claudius Caesar Emperor, that I have assuredly, honestly and truthfully presented the preceding return of those living with me, neither a stranger, Alexandrian nor freedman, nor Roman, nor Egyptian, except the aforesaid. If I am swearing truly may it be well with me, if falsely the opposite.

The second document is dated something like a century later, and it is chosen because it speaks of a woman who, like Mary, if tradition is correct, must have been a mere girl

when her son was born. Tausiris was thirty-four when her
son is returned as aged seventeen:

> To Julius Saturninus, officer of the Heracleopolite nome,
> from Petesouchos son of Pisiotis of the village of Ancyronon.
> I make my return in the 9th year of Antoninus Caesar, the
> lord, in accordance with the order of Valerius Proclus the
> prefect. Myself, Petesouchos aged 42, my wife Tausiris daugh-
> ter of Pareitis, aged 34, Pnephorus my son aged 17. I swear
> by the fortune of the emperor that I have presented the afore-
> said return honestly and truthfully and have told no lie nor
> omitted anyone who ought to have been returned by me, nor
> taken an advantage of identity of names. Otherwise may I
> endure the consequences of the oath.

The Birth Certificate

At the same time Joseph had another document to fill in
for the satisfaction of a bureaucratic age. It was a notifica-
tion of birth. Many of these documents survive, and the one
chosen speaks of a young mother with a husband very con-
siderably older than herself. It dates from the year A.D. 150:

> To Socrates and Didymus scribes of the metropolis from
> Ischyras son of Protas son of Mysthes, his mother being
> Tasoucharion, daughter of Didas, of the district of Hermonth-
> race, and from his wife Thiasarion, daughter of Ammonius,
> son of Mysthes of the same district. We register the son who
> was born to us, Ischyras, being one year of age in the present
> year, the 14th, of Antoninus Caesar the lord. I therefore pre-
> sent this notification of birth. Ischyras, aged 44, without dis-
> tinguishing marks. Thiasarion, aged 24 without distinguishing
> marks. Written for them by Ammonius, public scribe.

A second registration of birth dated exactly a century
earlier, in A.D. 50, may be added. It runs:

> To Arius son of Lysimachus, comogrammateus of Tebtunis,
> from Psoiphis son of Harpocras son of Pakebkis, his mother
> being Thenmarsisuchus daughter of Psoithis and Kellauthis,
> inhabitants of the village, priest of the fifth tribe of the gods
> at the village, Cronos, the most great god, and Isis and Sarapis,
> the great gods, and one of the fifty exempted persons. I register

Pakebkis, the son born to me and Taasies daughter of . . . and Taopis in the 10th year of Tiberius Claudius Caesar Augustus Germanicus Imperator, and request that the name of my aforesaid son Pakebkis be entered on the list. . . .

The papyrus is mutilated but the above gives the general sense. Psoiphis was "exempted" presumably from taxes, as a priest in office. The boy was "entered on the list" as an aspirant for the priesthood. It is possible that the father of John the Baptist completed some such document.

The Enrollment — An Historian's Note

These ancient relics of officialdom will suggest the atmosphere of Bethlehem on the night of the Nativity. As the returning people of the town sat around David's Well to renew old acquaintance and exchange tales of life abroad, there would be much fierce talk of Rome. Palestine was a turbulent province, and in many hearts smoldered that fierce resentment which blazed out sixty years later into the fire and passion of the Great Rebellion — a savage and hopeless struggle against the might of the Empire, which ended only with the destruction of Jerusalem, and the decimation of a race. Christ was born in occupied territory, and anyone, who would understand what men were thinking in the world to which He came, must take that fact into account. Men and women have not changed essentially in two thousand years, and the bitter experience of alien rule was a commonplace of life in the world of the first century. "O little town of Bethlehem," runs the carol, "how still we see thee lie." Bethlehem was anything but quiet on that crowded night.

These documents have something more than human interest. In the course of this book we shall have frequent occasion to mention the life and work of William Mitchell Ramsay. He it was who, convinced by his studies in the Acts of the Apostles that Luke the Evangelist was an historian of first-rate integrity and accuracy, set out to establish the historical truth of the complex of events surrounding the Nativity.

"Obviously," he wrote in his remarkable book *Was Christ Born at Bethlehem?*, "the story of Luke One and Two can never be demonstrated. There will always remain a large step to be taken in faith. . . . But it is highly important to show that the circumstances with which Luke connects this marvelous event are true, and that, in things which can be tested, he does not fall below the standard of accuracy demanded of ordinary historians."[3]

This Ramsay proceeded to do. The decree which illustrates the obligation under which the Holy Family found themselves to proceed to their ancestral hometown of Bethlehem, has already been quoted. Ramsay made use of the enrollment returns to establish the fourteen year rhythm of the Roman census, and to show that an enrollment took place in Palestine between the years 9 and 6 B.C.

The problem of the earlier governorship of Quirinius remains, and is not one which archaeology can solve. Inscriptions, none the less, locate Quirinius in office in Syria and Cilicia during the vital years, and offer a framework of conjecture into which Luke's story can convincingly fit. The matter is outside our present theme. Those curious to follow the argument which plausibly dates the birth of Christ in the autumn of 5 B.C. may find it set out in an appendix to *The Century of the New Testament.*[4] The amazing feature of the dating of the era is that a scheme first introduced in A.D. 525 should approach so close to the true date after an interval of five centuries.[5]

---

[3] Op. cit., pp. 112, 113.
[4] Pp. 147-151. By E. M. Blaiklock (Tyndale Press).
[5] A. J. Toynbee, *The Study of History*, Vol. VII p. 298.

ARCHAEOLOGY AND THE PARABLES

CHAPTER 3

ARCHAEOLOGY
AND THE PARABLES

THERE ARE FEW WORKS OF LITERATURE SURVIVING FROM the first century, which give a clear view of life as it was lived among the common people of the Empire. A large portion of the New Testament was written during the principate of Nero, A.D. 54-68, and, if the extant writings of those fifteen years are considered, the odd fact emerges that the only book which gives a vivid picture of common life was a story by Gaius Petronius, nicknamed Arbiter from his Beau Nash vocation as a dictator of elegance in Nero's court. Tacitus gives an account of this voluptuary, an aristocrat not unknown to the modern world from Henryk Sienkiewicz's brilliant portrait in his novel, *Quo Vadis*.

Petronius once governed Bithynia with energy and effi-ciency, and might have met Paul had he succeeded in visiting that province, but nothing is known of this more reputable activity. He is rather known as the indolent director of the young Nero's pleasures, and as the author of the *Satiricon*, a picaresque novel unlike anything else in Latin Literature. Large fragments survive. They tell of the disreputable doings

of three Greek scamps on the Campanian coast. Oddly
enough, if a comparison between works so disparate may
be hazarded, Petronius' satire, Columella's De Re Rustica,
parts of the New Testament, and especially Luke's two books,
must be bracketed as the only surviving publications of
Nero's principate which consistently give some indication of
a section of society outside the capital.

Petronius' novel shows the common life of that age of
money-making and vulgarity, of low crime and shattered
morality, among the poor and the undeservedly rich, in the
market place and the slums of Italian ports. The reader
becomes aware of the Roman proletariat, of a populace about
its petty business and varied carnality, remote from the
Palatine and aristocratic vice. It is a world glimpsed briefly
in the Pompeian *graffiti*, in the Egyptian papyri, and here
and there in the gospel parables.

It is interesting to draw papyri and parables together,
observe how true to authentic life the New Testament is, and
to understand in the process why "the common people heard
him gladly." Three parables will serve as illustration, and
the first is the most famous of all, the Parable of the Prodigal
Son — or is it rather of the Waiting Father?

The Parable of the Prodigal Son

If the account is read aright, it appears that Christ was
still teaching in Galilee on His last journey to Jerusalem. The
map makes the situation astonishingly clear, for if ever He
told a tale from life He told it here. The Lake of Tiberias, a
long blue basin in the valley, divides Galilee with its rolling
hills from the crowded Decapolis, in whose ten towns, from
Damascus down to Amman, Gentiles jostled with Jews. The
caravan routes around the Fertile Crescent curved that way,
and the cosmopolitan towns were ebullient with alien life, as
different from Galilee as Athens was remote from Jerusalem.

To catch some flavor of that vivid world, the visitor
should look at Gerasa, not Damascus or Amman. The modern

cities are alive and contemporary. A Roman theater, to be sure, stands in the midst of Amman's business quarter, perfectly preserved, and a magnificent memorial to the Philadelphia of the Ten Towns. Gerasa, modern Jerash, is a ruin, one of the most imposing ruins of the ancient world, an oval forum completely ringed with pillars, and a high-lifted theater, from which the audience on the stone seats could look over the heads of the actors down the pillared porticoes of a long and lovely boulevard, tall temples, houses, shops. They stand a solid stone memorial to the city to which the boy from Galilee could have come on foot in a couple of days. "He went into a far country and wasted his substance in riotous living." Miles do not matter. It was a country far enough, if its common way of life was set beside the quiet dignity of the old-fashioned household in Galilee.

Some itinerant Greek sophist, no doubt, had persuaded the lad that the Hebrew Scriptures sought to put the unknowable into words, that nothing indeed could be known

AT GERASA, *modern Jerash, many ruins are preserved. Among them are these columns on the east wing of the forum. The lighter shade at the base of the columns indicates the height of the earth removed by excavators.*

that the senses could not tell us, that obviously life is physical experience, and that Gerasa offered scope and opportunity. What he did not tell him was that the capacity of the body is limited, if its responses and reactions alone are the source of pleasure, that today's philosophy is discredited tomorrow, and that by weaving words philosophy can argue itself out of argument, and destroy by words the validity of the words in which it communicates. The same Greek doubtless aided his cynical townsmen to fleece the country boy from around the lake.

Meanwhile the father waited. The view is wide from the Galilean uplands above the Jordan valley. The upper end of the fertile river plain is visible, tessellated brown and green and gold. The river, a blue sinuous line, winds south. The lake is a level floor to the east and north. The father often watched the road winding down the hill slope to the river. And he saw him one day "afar off," limping home in rags, "and he ran and fell on his neck and kissed him." The wait was over, but not the pain. There was an elder brother, meticulous in conduct, but merciless, jealous, and without an inkling of what went on in his father's mind, the very picture of the Pharisees whom Christ had in view. In Gerasa's oval forum they would have shuddered in their purple-bordered robes to jostle Greeks and caravaneers from the Persian Gulf. They knew all the rules of religion, every subtle detail of the Law, but knew no mercy, no care for the outcast, the underprivileged, the alien.

From the rainless sands south of Cairo, where papyrus lies undamaged in the sand and does not rot, comes a letter written at the turn of the first century by a boy named Antonius Longus to Nilous his mother. It runs pathetically after its formal opening:

Antonius Longus to Nilous, his mother, greeting. Continually I pray for your health. I had no hope that you would come up to town. On this account I did not enter the city either. I was ashamed to come for I am going about in rags. I beseech you, mother, forgive me. I know what I have brought upon myself. I have been punished, in any case. I know that I have sinned. . . . .

. . . "I will arise and go to my father and say unto him, "Father, I have sinned and am no more worthy to be called your son . . ."

All prodigals did not come home, nor, if they ventured back, found such a father as the one chosen by the Lord to show forth the love of God. Here, for example, is a public notice from the first or second century:

To Heracleides, strategos of the Hermapolite name, from Ammonius the elder, the son of Ermaeus, and his former wife A . . . along with her present husband Callistratus . . . Since our son Castor, along with others, by riotous living has squandered all his own property, and now has laid hands on ours and desires to scatter it, on that account we are taking precautions lest he should deal despitefully with us or do anything else amiss . . . We beg therefore that a proclamation be set up (that no one should lend him money.)

There are many such documents among the papyri, some of them almost savage in their expression of deep resentment against wayward children. The following, for example, is part of a deed of disownment in which a father cast off two sons and two daughters:

Thinking to find you a comfort to my age, submissive and obedient, you in your prime have set yourselves against me like rancorous beings. Wherefore I reject and abhor you. . . .

The document runs on with legal abuse for some five hundred words. If the papyri are any indication, the father who killed the fatted calf for his lost boy's returning was gracious beyond custom of that ancient world.

How Nilous received the despairing letter in A.D. 100 is not known. The Jewish father was waiting, watching the valley below. And life is often like that. If it is an opportunity for mercy, large-heartedness, pity, and generosity, which stumbles up the road, let us not be gruff, mean-minded, cynical.

The Parable of the Dishonest Steward

A second parable, which finds similar illustration, is that of the steward who lost his post. The story is told in Luke 16, and ends with words which some have misunderstood. "And the lord commended the unjust steward because he had done wisely." The lord who thus praised the dishonest fellow is not the Lord Jesus. He has no capital L. He was the steward's own lord, his master, his employer. Rich enough to laugh at the loss of a few barrels of oil and wine, the owner dropped some words of rueful praise for the smart dealing of which he was the victim. And this is the parable's point: the rogue of the world will leave no stone unturned to gain his end. The world will watch and grimly praise him, as he turns the world's resources to his purpose. What of this enterprise in a nobler sphere? Cannot Christians scheme as indefatigably for the kingdom's sake? "Make friends," the Lord concluded, "by means of the Mammon of Unrighteousness." If rascals can use money to build themselves comfort, cannot others use it for God?

From the Egyptian papyri quite a band of scoundrels in office can be assembled. It was a highly regimented age, and in Egypt especially, where an ancient fiscal system had been taken over by the Greeks first and then by the Romans, the ramifications of taxation and Governmental control were modern in their complexity. Documents, reports, statements, deeds, receipts and all the paraphernalia of business and bureaucracy, were part of Egypt's way of life. Here are three to illustrate the point.

The first is a complaint of petty theft on a demolition job, dated from the year of the Crucifixion and Resurrection of Christ:

> To Serapion, chief of police, from Orsenouphis son of Harp-aesis, notable of the village of Euhemeria in the division of Themistes. In the month Mesore of the past 14th year of Tiberius Caesar I was having some old walls on my premises demolished by the mason Petesouchus, son of Petesouchus, and

while I was absent from home to gain my living, Petesouchus, in the process of demolition, discovered a hoard which had been secreted by my mother in a little box as long ago as the 16th year of Augustus Caesar, consisting of a pair of gold earrings weighing 4 quarters, a gold crescent weighing 3 quarters, a pair of silver armlets of the weight of 12 drachmae of uncoined metal, a necklace with silver ornaments worth 80 drachmae, and 60 silver drachmae. Diverting the attention of his assistants and my people, he had them conveyed to his own home by his maiden daughter, and after emptying out the aforesaid objects he threw away the box empty in my house, and he even admitted finding the box, though he pretends that it was empty. Wherefore I request, if you approve, that the accused be brought before you for the consequent punishment. Farewell.

Orsenouphis, aged 50, scar on left forearm.

THIS PAPYRUS LETTER, *typical of Bible times, is rolled, tied, and sealed.*

The second is an order on a bank dated A.D. 99. The New Testament canon had just been rounded off by John:

Aphrodous daughter of Satyrus, with her kinsman Ammonius son of Heraclides as guardian, to Sambas also called Didymus, banker, greeting. Pay to Charition also called Tasoucharion daughter of Charidemus and to Charition daughter of Didymus, each with her husband as guardian, Charition also called Tasoucharion with Apollonius and the other Charition with Heron son of Didymus, as the price of a half share of a house and courtyard and offices and all the appurtenances in the village of Theadelphia in the division of Themistes in accordance with the . . . . deeds of conveyance made with them, the six hundred silver drachmae of mine which you hold on deposit, total 600 dr. The 2nd year of the Emperor Caesar Nerva Trajanus Augustus Germanicus, Tubi 28. (Receipted) I, Charition daughter of Didymus, with my husband Heron son of Didymus as guardian, bid this be filed, and I have received the three hundred silver drachmae falling to my share, total 300 dr. I, Heron, have written for my wife also, as she is illiterate. The 2nd year of the Emperor Caesar Nerva Trajanus Augustus Germanicus, Tubi 28, I, Charition also called Tasoucharion daughter of Charidemus, with my husband Apollonius son of Apion as guardian, have received the three hundred drachmae, total 300 dr. I, Apollonius, having written for my wife also, as she is illiterate.

In the third and final illustration of the documentary preoccupation of that paper-ridden age, consider a deed of apprenticeship to a weaver, dated A.D. 183:

Tryphon son of Dionysius son of Tryphon and of Thamounis daughter of Onnophris, and Ptolemaeus son of Pausirion son of Ptolemaeus and of Ophelous daughter of Theon, weaver, both being inhabitants of Oxyrhynchus, mutually acknowledge that Tryphon has apprenticed to Ptolemaeus his son Thoonis, whose mother is Saraeus daughter of Apion, and who is not yet of age, for a period of one year from the present day, to serve and to follow all the instructions given to him by Ptolemaeus in the art of weaving as far as he himself knows it, the boy to be fed and clothed for the whole period by his father Tryphon, who will also be responsible for all taxes on him, on the condition that Ptolemaeus will pay to him monthly on account of food 5 drachmae and at the close of the whole period on account of clothing 12 drachmae, nor shall Tryphon have the right to remove the boy from Ptolemaeus until the completion of the period, and for whatever days therein the boy plays truant, he shall send him to work for the like number at the end of it, or else forfeit one drachma of silver for each day, and for removing him within the period he shall pay a penalty of 100 drachmae and the like sum to the Treasury. If Ptolemaeus fails to instruct the boy fully, he shall be liable to the same penalties. This contract of apprenticeship is valid. The

13th year of Nero Claudius Ceasar Augustus Germanicus Imperator, the 21st of the month Sebastus. (Signed) I, Ptolemaeus son of Pausirion son of Ptolemaeus and of Ophelous daughter of Theon, will do everything in the one year. I, Zoilus son of Horus son of Zoilus and of Dieus daughter of Sokeus have written for him, as he is illiterate. The 13th year of Nero Claudius Caesar Augustus Germanicus Imperator, Sebastus 21.

It is a sad comment on human nature that such societies produce graft and offer unbounded opportunities for the nefarious activities of such scoundrels as the Unjust Steward and the tax-collectors of the gospels. One such man is known to the modern world from a letter file discovered by Grenfell and Hunt in a crocodile cemetery at Tebtunis. The crocodile was sacred in Egypt, and on demise received honorable burial. Sick of finding the dry carcasses where he had hoped for sarcophagi and baksheesh, a workman smashed one open with his pick, and revealed that it was stuffed with waste papyri. Most of the documents were official records, and Menches' note was among them. This is what Menches wrote:

> On being appointed to the post of town clerk, I will pay at the village 50 artabae of wheat, and 50 artabae of pulse, namely, 20 of lentils and 10 of bruised beans, 6 of mixed seed, 10 of peas, 3 of mustard and 1 of parched pulse: total 100 artabae.

Now the office he sought was honorary. Here he offers payment, and his letter mentions no recipient and bears no date. Menches' undertaking to cultivate certain land is also mentioned in a document in his file. It is dated 119 B.C. and runs:

> Asclepiades to Marres greeting. Menches having been appointed by the dioecetes to the village secretaryship of Kerkeosiris on the understanding that he shall cultivate at his own expense ten arurae of the land in the area of the village which has been reported as unproductive, at a rent of fifty artabae, to the Government in full, or else make up the deficiency from his private means, give to him the papers of

his office and take care that the terms of his undertaking are fulfilled. Goodbye. Year 51, Mesore 3. (Addressed) To Marres, district secretary.

Why was Menches so eager to hold his petty office? Simpler men were eager to escape the honorary burden. We may read, for example, the pathetic appeal of a doctor who found himself saddled with a local magistracy:

After toiling for four years at my post, (he wrote) I am become very run down, my lord. I entreat you, my preserver, have pity, and order me to be released from my duties. Add instructions, please, that those practicing medicine be granted exemption, especially those who, like myself, have passed the examinations.

Why then did Menches want the post? Reading between the faded lines in the private letters of the age we gather that an official could often turn a shady drachma. Consider for example, this letter of A.D. 200;

Ammonius to Apion, greetings. If you can, buy up all the peaches on the market. Don't neglect it, for if the gods will, the Government is about to market them. Don't be faint-hearted. Manage this so that peaches can be bought through you alone, and know that you will not suffer as far as I am concerned.

It is curious that what is probably the first mention of peaches in all literature, should also introduce us to a bureaucratic marketing scheme, and to a shady plot to corner the crop. It was an advantage to Apion to have a friend like Ammonius in an official position!

Bad man Menches may have looked for more than inside information on marketing legislation. All the village taxes would pass through his hands. He would be registrar, too, of all trades and properties. "A certain Artemidorus, scribe of Ciris," complains a lady named Seniphibis, "has registered me as having more land than I possess, and in consequence inflicts much loss on me." "The collection of corn dues," complains another, in A.D. 215, "is based on obsolete lists of names, and the collections are involving injustice to many."

Both documents give us a glimpse of a thoroughly corrupt bureaucracy. Menches, too, would deal with all applications for rent rebates. A burning question, as early as the first century, was the just rate of rebate for Government tenants in years when the flooding of the Nile proved disappointing. The bureaucrats seem never to have succeeded in establishing a workable sliding scale. Tiberius Julius Alexander, in the late first century, condemned the practice of basing rents on a past average, but as late as Hadrian we find the problem still worrying officialdom.

In both Greek and Roman times everything one did or ate in Egypt was taxed. Hermaiscus opened a vegetable shop in Broad Street at Pson in A.D. 222, and we have the receipt for his registration fee. All the other shops in Broad Street, and every trade, suffered like infliction. It even cost a handful of good drachmae to die, for there was a tax on grave-digging. There must have been pickings for men like Menches, if they "walked on their feet in the market place," to use the quaint term which appears in declarations of testamentary capacity.

It must have been annoying for a temperamental painter seeking to catch a glow of sunset, to have Menches assess his canvas, but, oddly enough, there was a tax on paintings. What an opportunity when a grandee passed through on the way to the Pyramids, and food and transport had to be requisitioned! It was well for the farmer next door to be the town clerk's friend, even at the expense of "31 dishes and one meal bowl," which Pachon took to the pawnshop on "the 10th" of an undecipherable month and year.

Here for example is a letter from Menches' own decade, dated 112 B.C., which must have made the petty official who received it groan. The end of the letter is too mutilated to read the list of "gifts mentioned below." It might also be noted that Petesouchus was a crocodile-God, and that the Labyrinth is the temple beside the pyramid of Amenemhet III at Hawara. Here is the text:

Hermias to Horus greeting. Below is a copy of the letter to Asclepiades. Take care then that instructions are followed. Goodbye. Year 5, Xandious 17, Mecheir 17.

To Asclepiades. Lucius Memmius, a Roman senator, who occupies a position of great dignity and honor, is sailing up from Alexandria to the Arsinoite nome to see the sights. Let him be received with special magnificence, and take care that at the proper spots the guest-chambers be prepared and the landing-places to them be completed, and that the furniture of the guest-chamber, the tidbits for Petesouchus and the crocodiles, the conveniences for viewing the Labyrinth, and the offerings and sacrifices be provided. In general take the greatest pains in everything to see that the visitor is satisfied, and display the utmost zeal.

The accounts, of course, were audited. But what then? A letter from Menches' hoard reads: "Polemon to Menches, greeting. The inspector from the Treasury will pass your village on the 16th, so try to have all arrears in order." Another official writes: "The inspector of temple finance is here. Write up your books and come to me, for he is a very stern fellow. If anything detains you, send them on and I will see you through, for he has become my friend."

Here is a letter from just such a "stern fellow," not from Menches' file, but from A.D. 23:

Apollonius, strategus, to Akous, toparch of Tebtunis, greeting. Send me at once a supplementary classified statement of payments made up to date; for I shall judge by this whether I shall leave you on duty where you are, or summon you and send you to the prefect for neglect of the collecting. Goodbye. The ninth year of Tiberius Caesar Augustus, Mecheir 21. (Addressed) To Akous, toparch of Tebtunis.

It is obvious that the trickster and grafter of the Lord's pungent little parable was no isolated type. The crumbling documents from the Tebtunis crocodile provide realistic illustration both of the racy story, and the Teller's didactic method. The parables were contemporary, relevant and intimate.

The Parable of the Wheat and the Tares

For the third and final illustration consider the earlier parable from the ministry in Galilee — the Wheat and the Tares. . . .

It must have been somewhere in the vicinity of the year A.D. 250 when a family group attended at the local town clerk's office in the little Egyptian town of Theadelphia. The systematic persecution with which a dying paganism was afflicting the Church was at its height, and the long arm of the Emperor Decius was seeking out the Christians by the Nile.

An accommodating Government had made it possible for those so disposed to avoid all penalty by renouncing Christ. Pliny, the governor of Bithynia, whom we shall meet again, writing to the Emperor Trajan in A.D. 110, had first laid down the practice.[1] The letter survives, and the mode of procedure, in Pliny's words, was this:

> In the meanwhile, the method I have observed towards those who have been denounced to me as Christians is this: I interrogated them whether they were Christians; if they confessed it I repeated the question twice again, adding the threat of capital punishment; if they still persevered, I ordered them to be executed. For whatever the nature of their creed might be, I could at least feel no doubt that contumacy and inflexible obstinacy deserved chastisement. There were others also possessed with the same infatuation, but being citizens of Rome, I directed them to be carried thither.
>
> These accusations spread (as is usually the case) from the mere fact of the matter being investigated, and several forms of the mischief came to light. A placard was put up, without any signature, accusing a large number of persons by name. Those who denied they were, or had ever been, Christians, who repeated after me an invocation to the gods, and offered adoration, with wine and frankincense, to your image, which I had ordered to be brought for that purpose, together with those of the gods, and who finally cursed Christ — none of which acts, it is said, those who are really Christians can be

---

[1] *Epistles* 10:96.

forced into performing — these I thought it proper to discharge. Others who were named by that informer at first confessed themselves Christians, and then denied it; true, they had been of that persuasion but they had quitted it, some three years, others many years, and a few as much as twenty-five years ago. They all worshipped your statue and the images of the gods, and cursed Christ.

As in Bithynia, so it was in Theadelphia. One of the more somber parables of the Lord was finding illustration. The wheat and the tares grow together, and it is only the Day of Judgment which separates the true from the false, and the genuine from its imitation. And the Day of Judgment is sometimes the coming of persecution, and the sword of authority outstretched against that which challenges its baseness, and recognizes, beyond all earthly might, the power of the living God. In such times the weak and unconvinced fall off, and they alone remain whose faith is true, and who count all things, even life itself, as loss for Christ.

Pliny in the letter already quoted, reports succcess for his policy of moderation, for so he imagined it. "The contagious superstition" of which he disapproved, was clearly checked. He wrote:

It is certain at least that the temples, which had been almost deserted, begin now to be frequented; and the sacred festivals, after a long intermission, are again revived; while there is a general demand for sacrificial meat, which for some time past had met with but few purchasers. From hence it is easy to imagine that multitudes may be reclaimed from this error, if a door be left open to repentance.

We have left meanwhile a little group from the Theadelphian church waiting the petty magistrate's pleasure outside the governmental office in the Egyptian town. Several of them were members of one family, who had in some past year adopted the Emperor's name. They were there to sign documents which repudiated their Christian faith, they and others to the number of at least nineteen, whose writings of recantation were discovered in 1904 and 1907 among the papyri. This is what the Aurelian family read and signed with appropriate witnesses:

> To the superintendents of offerings and sacrifices at the city. From Aurelius . . . . . son of Theodorius and Pantonymis of the said city. It has ever been my custom to make sacrifices and pour libations to the gods and now also I have in your presence in accordance with the commandment poured libations, made sacrifice and tasted the offerings, together with my son Aurelius Dioscuros and my daughter Aurelia Lais. I therefore request you to certify my statement.

A second document runs:

> To those chosen to have charge of the sacrifices, from Aurelia, wife of Ammonarios, from the village Theadelphia, and who always sacrifices and reverences the gods, together with the children of the Aurelian family, Didymos and Nouphios and Taat.

> We have ever continued to sacrifice and to reverence the gods with the children of the Aurelians, Didymos and Nouphios, and now in your presence according to the orders we have poured libations and have sacrificed and have tasted of the sacrifices, and I demand of you that you witness this with your signature for me. Farewell.

Another of these strange documents, published in 1907, was held by a pagan priestess. "Aurelia Ammonous Mystos, priestess of Petesouchos, the great god" was her description. Since it is unlikely that a priestess would be wrongly accused of Christianity, it is fair to guess that Aurelia had become a Christian, and then recanted under threat of punishment.

Such is the illustration of the Parable of the Wheat and Tares which archaeology has been able to supply.

ARCHAEOLOGY AND THE
SAYINGS OF CHRIST

CHAPTER 4

ARCHAEOLOGY
AND THE SAYINGS OF CHRIST

THERE ARE OTHER WORDS OF CHRIST WHICH FIND THEIR way into few sermons. They have come to light, a scanty and unproven heritage, from strange sources outside the pages of Scripture, but often with the marks of truth upon them. Two of the most remarkable non-biblical sayings of Christ, for example, are preserved by Moslems, one in an ode of the poet Nizami and the other woven into the arabesques above the gateway of an Indian mosque. Both carry a subtle flavor of authenticity.

The Moslem Record

One evening, says the Mohammedan poet, Jesus came into the crowded marketplace. A crowd was gathered, as idle orientals will, about some object of interest in a corner, and the Master, coming up unobserved, saw a dead dog at their feet. It was a revolting sight. The dog in the ancient east was the object of loathing and contempt. "Am I a dead dog?" one asked in anger at insult or derision. And there was a dead dog. And more than dead. The animal's ribs were

bare, its ears torn, its ragged hide stained black with mud
and blood. A frayed and filthy end of rope was about its
neck. Jesus stood unobserved behind the group and heard
their disgusted comments on the ugly sight. "His eyes are
blear. His ears are foul. His ribs are bare." Then quietly He
said, "Pearls cannot rival the whiteness of his teeth." Men
turned startled and rebuked. "This," said someone, "must be
Jesus of Nazareth." The tribute was eloquent enough. He
had a way of saying things which burned the heart. One remembers another famous story. "Let him that is without sin
among you throw the first stone." And as He waited, writing
with a finger in the sand, the accusers, their spirits stripped
bare before Him, dropped their stones and slunk away. The
saying recorded in the Moslem poet is a genuine echo.

In a town twenty-four miles west of Agra is a big mosque
with a magnificent gateway one hundred and twenty feet
high and broad. In the scrolled decorations of doorposts and
plinth an Arabic sentence is written. It runs: "Jesus, on
whom be peace, said, 'The world is merely a bridge, you are
to pass over it, and not to build your dwellings upon it.'"
How came the saying to the Indian mosque? There is a
tradition, so strong as to be almost certainly true, that
Thomas and Bartholomew preached the Gospel in India.
There is a strong and ancient branch of the Indian Church
which antedates modern missionary enterprise. This Christian community Akbar found, when he took up the reins of
India. Akbar was an enlightened Moslem. Like the Roman
Emperor Severus, who had statues of Abraham, Christ and
Orpheus, along with the pagan deities, in his private chapel,
Akbar tried to fuse the religions of his realm, and even
invited a Portuguese missionary from Goa to preach there.
The saying of Christ over a mosque which Akbar founded is
a relic of this policy.

What did the saying mean? The only river in Palestine
is the Jordan, and it is crossed not by bridges but by fords.
Where did the Lord, who always linked His teaching to

known, familiar things, see a bridge? It is recorded in the gospels that He once preached at Tyre. Tyre in those days was a sorry ruin of the mighty commercial city of the Phoenicians who held Cyprus, founded Carthage, sent ships to India and Britain, and supplied the master-builders with the great cedar beams for Solomon's temple in Jerusalem. Tyre was an island until, more than three centuries before Christ, Alexander came. In the pride of her strength Tyre closed her gates, and bade the Greek do his worst.

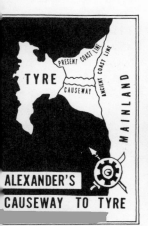

THE CITY OF TYRE, *with a view of its ancient main street. The map illustrates the causeway formed by the land-bridge built by Alexander the Great, three centuries before Christ, connecting the island city to the ancient coastline.*

Alexander responded with his usual dynamic energy. He built a causeway across the water, took his engines and assault troops across to the walls and stormed the city. The causeway, widened by the drifting sands to a full quarter of a mile, exists still. In Christ's day, it still had the appearance of a bridge. Was it in this connection that Christ uttered His words? The causeway of Tyre was a road to somewhere. No one, as on old London Bridge, built houses on it. So, according to the saying, is life. We have here "no continuing city."

Like Abraham we "look for a city which hath foundations." In search of it we wander like nomads.

The Exclusion From the Gospels

It has always been known, apart from such chance records, that much which Christ said and did found no place in the brief records of the gospels. In one version of Luke's gospel, one such lost saying, a striking remark on the Sabbath, actually intruded. Who slipped it into the Codex Bezae is not known, but it runs thus: "On the same day, seeing someone working on the Sabbath, He said to him: Man, if you know what you are doing, blessed you are. If you do not know you are accursed, and a transgressor of the law." It is odd that more such sayings did not find their way into the text, for John himself remarked that he "supposed the world would not hold the books" if the whole story were told. Paul quotes "the saying of the Lord Jesus, 'It is more blessed to give than to receive,'" and the saying is not in the record of the Evangelists. Luke, too, speaks of "many who have taken in hand to draw up a narrative," and tradition has it that Matthew, before he wrote his gospel, made a collection of sayings of Christ. There is stranger confirmation. In his spirited history of the Third Crusade, the French knight De Joinville, who himself swung his sword for Saint Louis, tells the story of a brave monk. High up in the Lebanon Ranges lived the Old Man of the Mountain, and Brother Peter was sent by the French king with a message to him. The King was, in point of fact, uneasy. The Old Man kept a secret police. He doped its desperadoes with hashish made from hemp, and sent them out with daggers to interfere by assassination in foreign affairs. From the name of the drug they were termed "hashashin" whence, as one may guess, the English word "assassins." When the monk arrived at the Old Man's stronghold, no mean act of courage, he found the ancient scoundrel with a book by his bed. It was "the words of the Lord unto Peter," and it is a pity he failed to secure a copy. Such collections, then, existed in A.D. 1248 in the Syrian hills.

The Papyrus Evidence

It was not until the end of the nineteenth century that the first papyrus sheet came to light. Two of its sayings ring amazingly true. Said the Lord to an ancient audience: "Thou hearest with one ear, but the other thou hast closed." He might say it still. The other saying was a word for the lonely: "Wherever there are two they are not without God, and if one is alone anywhere I say that I am with him. Raise the stone, there thou shalt find Me: cleave the wood and there I am." What did He mean by those last words? Did He mean that a Christian faith, that God's grace and purpose, could sanctify and glorify the toil of the humblest, the hewers of wood and drawers of water, "the scorned and rejected, the men hemmed in with spears"? Or did He mean that the cloven log and the river-washed stone are full of the wonder of the Creator's hand for the eyes that are open to see? The meaning of such sayings need not be limited. This one takes its place among the world's wise words.

From a second sheet of sayings found in 1904 another word may be chosen. It runs, "Let him who seeks cease not till he finds, and when he finds he shall be astonished; astonished he shall reach the Kingdom, and having reached the Kingdom he shall rest." An ancient tradition retains another saying of Christ which similarly links wonder and spiritual progress. "Wonder at the things before you," it makes Him say and comment: "This is the first step to the knowledge that lies beyond." The saying links Jesus with Plato, who said: "The mark of a philosopher is this — wonder." And how true! James Watt "wondered" about a kettle, Newton about an apple, Archimedes about a bath — and science leaped forward. Life can only be true and meaningful with wonder. The Kingdom of God is for those who seek. In the wonder of it, in E. B. Browning's phrase, "every common bush" is ablaze with Him, while "the rest sit round it and pick blackberries." Wonder is the mark of the questing soul who treads the highway to truth, and "astonishment" is his reward.

The Treasure in Earthen Vessels

"This treasure," wrote Saint Paul in a well-known passage, "we have in earthen vessels." He was referring to the storing or concealing of valuables in sealed jars, a practice of which the Qumran Scrolls provide illustration. Similarly hidden was a parcel of papyri unearthed at Naj Hamadi, between Cairo and Luxor, late in 1945.

THESE EARTHEN VESSELS FROM QUMRAN *illustrate the types of vessels in which many valuable manuscripts were found.*

The fact that the contents did at last reach the West, full fourteen years after a large clay jar was unearthed by fellahin digging near the site of a fourth-century monastery, was due to a Belgian scholar, Gilles Quispel. It was his enterprise and patience which found its way through the sinuosities of the lamentable black market in antiquities, and persuaded the jealous librarians of Egypt to release information which they most reprehensibly withheld.

The major treasure in the earthen vessel from Naj Hamadi, was the so-called *Gospel of Thomas,* some inkling of which had appeared in a papyrus find of Grenfell and Hunt in 1903. The document is a collection of one hundred and fourteen sayings of Jesus, in the form of isolated dicta or brief conversations, some known, some entirely new.

Like the logia of earlier discovery, the sayings from the Naj Hamadi papyrus must be judged on their merits. Some are inconsiderable, and contain none of the edge and patina so characteristic of the biblical utterances of Christ. Others, on the contrary, are fresh and pungent, and may represent a genuine tradition.

A few illustrations of the latter order will make the point clear. "Jesus said: Whoever is near to Me is near the fire, and whoever is far from Me is far from the kingdom." The

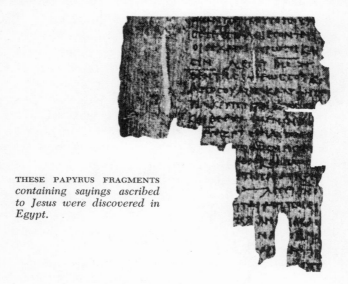

THESE PAPYRUS FRAGMENTS *containing sayings ascribed to Jesus were discovered in Egypt.*

words coincide with more than one warning from the Master
that true discipleship can lead to persecution and loss, but
that it is also true that the discovery of God lay in the acceptance of His lordship. "Whoever is near me, is near the fire,"
is a saying preserved by Origen.

It is a strange fact about Jesus Christ that, contrary to
every saintly character of common humanity, He never be-
trayed consciousness of sin in word, or thought, or act. He
faced His hostile critics calmly with the astounding challenge: "Which of you convinceth me of sin?" He looked
open-eyed to Almighty God and said: "I have glorified you
upon earth." It is striking to find in the sayings attributed to
Thomas a similar claim to sinlessness. "They said to Him:
'Come and let us pray today and let us fast.' Jesus said:
'Which then is the sin that I have committed, or in what have
I been vanquished?'" To meet such words is to be sharply
reminded of the superhuman psychology of One who could
so testify without arrogance, absurdity, or rapid refutation,
though admittedly there is not the full ring of truth about it.

Here is another striking saying: "Jesus said: 'Become
passers-by.'" The words in no sense commend the attitude
of the priest and Levite who passed the wounded man on the
Jericho road. It is in tune rather with the saying of Christ
already mentioned, preserved amid the arabesques of the
Moslem mosque: "Life is a bridge. You pass over it but build
no houses on it." These words likewise speak of Christian de-
tachment, the obligation to hold material things with a light
hand, the readiness for Christ's sake, to avoid involvement in
the tangle of worldly living, the willingness, in a word, to
set the eyes on the prize set before, and walk the mundane
path in the spirit in which the writer of the epistle to the
Hebrews bids his readers run the race.

Authenticity of the Sayings

All these sayings have the ring of authenticity. So do
such words as the new Beatitude: "Blessed is the man who

suffers. He finds life." And the reproach to the Pharisees:
"Woe to them, for they are like a dog sleeping in the manger
of oxen, for neither does he eat or allow the oxen to eat."
The figure of the dog in the manger is originally Greek, but
here is Christ quoting it in Palestine, and vividly, if one remembers the wolfish pariah curs of Palestine, and forgets the
sleek fox terrier of the well-known painting.

Some of the sayings reproduce those already known.
Sometimes they present a slightly worn appearance, like the
one about sinlessness already quoted, natural enough if one
remembers that the collection is dated about A.D. 140, almost
a half-century after the Canon of the New Testament closed.
Compare, for example, the well-known Parable of the Sower
and the Seed with this slightly blurred and attenuated version: "See, the sower went out, he filled his hand, he threw.
Some seed fell on the road, the birds came, they gathered
them. Others fell on the rock, and did not strike root in the
earth, and did not produce ears. And others fell on the thorns.
They choked the seed and the worm ate them. And others
fell on the good earth, and brought forth good fruit. It bore
sixty per measure, and one hundred and twenty per
measure." The closing words are a little obscure, but note
the Semitic method of counting . . . sixty, one hundred and
twenty. . . .

This is obviously a different tradition, held, no doubt, by
the Christian community which, according to tradition,
escaped from Jerusalem before its fall in A.D. 70, and quite
independent of that which is so richly represented in the
gospels. It is a remarkable testimony to the trustworthiness
of the Bible.

As a footnote let us place the pungent little parable of
the woman with the cracked jar. It is a Naj Hamadi comment on some of the pseudo-theologies of our day:

The Kingdom of the Father is like a woman who was carrying
a jar full of meal. While she was walking on a distant road
the handle of the jar broke. The meal streamed out behind

her on the road. She did not know it. She had noticed no accident. After she came into her house, she put the jar down and found it empty.

To carry the Bread of Life in a modern container is a fine idea, but we must be sure that the container is such that the contents are not lost.

ARCHAEOLOGY AND THE DEATH OF CHRIST

CHAPTER 5

ARCHAEOLOGY
AND THE DEATH OF CHRIST

In the drama of the Easter Story, Pilate stands with Judas in the villain's role. How temperament and circumstance forced him to that part is a tale worth telling, and one on which archaeology, or at least numismatics, can provide a comment.

It is a story difficult to piece together, for Pilate left no word of his own, nor found a friend to defend him. He was a stern and selfish man with few friends, no doubt, and many enemies, intractable, with an odd streak of cowardice, and the last man who should have been Governor of Palestine.

When he sat on the judgment seat that Easter morning at the place called the Pavement, Pilate was facing the fruits of folly. Pontius Pilate is mentioned by writers sacred and secular, Josephus, Philo, and the four Evangelists, and on all occasions he wins the right to reference by an act of obstinate folly. He had carried the legionary standards into Jerusalem with the medallions attached, and so, by setting up an idolatrous portrait in the holy place, stirred the hysterical anger of the Jews.

Pilate — An Historian's Testimony

The Jews, moreover, had beaten him on the issue. Josephus may be left to tell the story of the standards.

Pilate, (he writes) being sent by Tiberius as procurator to Judaea, introduced into Jerusalem by night and under cover the effigies of Caesar which are called standards. This proceeding, when day broke, aroused immense excitement among the Jews; those on the spot were in consternation, considering their laws to have been trampled under foot, as those laws permit no image to be erected in the city; while the indignation of the townspeople stirred the countryfolk who flocked together in crowds. Hastening after Pilate to Caesarea, the Jews implored him to remove the standards from Jerusalem and to uphold the laws of their ancestors. When Pilate refused, they fell prostrate around his house and for five whole days and nights remained motionless in that position.

On the ensuing day Pilate took his seat on his tribunal in the great stadium, and summoning the multitude with the apparent intention of answering them, gave the arranged signal to his armed soldiers to surround the Jews. Finding themselves in a ring of troops, three deep, the Jews were struck dumb at this unexpected sight. Pilate, after threatening to cut them down if they refused to admit Caesar's images, signalled to the soldiers to draw their swords. Thereupon the Jews, as by concerted action, flung themselves in a body on the ground, extended their necks, and exclaimed that they were ready to die rather than to transgress the Law. Overcome with astonishment at such religious zeal, Pilate gave orders for the immediate removal of the standards from Jerusalem.[1]

Now there is to be observed in this incident a certain blend of arrogance and cowardice. The ensigns, surmounted by an eagle and bearing Caesar's image, offended a Jewish prejudice based on the second commandment. Why was Pilate so provocative? Perhaps he clumsily sought to honor the dangerous old emperor. Perhaps he indulged a superstition of his own, which weighed more in his mind than a superstition of the Jews. At any rate, from beginning to end

---

[1] Josephus, *B. J.* II 8. 9.

the incident was a lesson and a demonstration to the Jews. They had summed up their governor, and knew that his arrogance could be overridden by clamor, and that his cowardice at a certain point asserted itself.

Some time later, if we are to believe Philo in a matter passed over by Josephus,[2] Pilate tried again, timidly or obstinately, to honor the emperor where he had not been honored before, in Jerusalem. In Herod's palace he hung some gilded votive shields dedicated to Tiberius. The reaction was violent. Pilate faced immediately a deputation of the Sanhedrin, and the four surviving sons of Herod the Great. The latter group, exploiting the influence which their family had always enjoyed in Rome, appealed to Caesar, when Pilate proved obdurate, and Tiberius sent a curt order to his governor to move the shields to Caesarea, and hang them in the temple of Augustus. It is easy to see why Pilate was shy of a further complaint, but he had handed another advantage to his foes.

A third incident shows the same gaucherie, the same mingling of cruelty and timidity, the same inability to cope with provincials. Josephus may again tell the story. The passage continues the chapter already quoted.

On a later occasion, (writes the historian) he provoked a fresh uproar by expending upon the construction of an aqueduct the sacred treasure known as *corbonas*. The water was brought from a distance of 400 furlongs. Indignant at this proceeding, the populace formed a ring around the tribunal of Pilate, then on a visit to Jerusalem, and besieged him with angry clamor. He, foreseeing the tumult, had interspersed among the crowd a troop of his soldiers, armed, but disguised in civilian dress, with orders not to use their swords, but to beat any rioters with cudgels. From his tribunal he gave the agreed signal. Large numbers of the Jews perished, some from the blows which they received, others trodden to death by their companions in the ensuing flight. Cowed by the fate of the victims, the multitude was reduced to silence.

[2] *Leg ad Gaium*, XXIII.

Pilate could clearly not afford another appeal to Caesar. It was dangerous to annoy further the old recluse of Capri. Add to the list of follies the sacrilegious massacre in Galilee mentioned in the gospels, and the sum of Pilate's mistakes assumes perilous proportions. Hence the triumph of the priests at the trial of Christ, and their victory over a man who was convinced of the evil of their accusations, and seeking a way within the limits of his cowardice and already compromised career, to follow justice and release the Prisoner. Pilate sinned that day because his past was too powerful.

Pilate's Coins

But why this policy of repression and folly? Perhaps another and even more sinister figure is partly to blame. Pilate was probably an appointee of Seianus, the powerful commander of the household troops in Rome, and for many years, until, in A.D. 31, the emperor found him out and struck him down, the trusted right-hand man of the dour Tiberius. Was Seianus an anti-Semitist, and did he recommend Pilate for the governorship of the turbulent province because he hated the Jews? Pilate, at any rate, appears to have adopted his provocative policy immediately, and not after frustration at his subjects' hands. And that is shown by his coinage, a source of evidence which cannot be overlooked. The procurators had the right to issue small coinage in the province of Palestine, but it was considered a duty, in designing coins which would be in the hands of multitudes, to avoid deliberate offense. Coins were always far more significant to their ancient users than they are today. They were a means of instruction and propaganda, were observed more closely, and studied for what they had to say. The modern postage stamp sometimes fulfills this purpose.

The story of Christ and the tribute money shows that the emperor's portrait, with the offense involved, was abroad in Palestine, but the silver denarius was actually issued as tribute money, and accepted as such by the legally-minded Jews. It was quite a different matter to deluge the land with common copper coinage which ran contrary to Jewish sentiment. Valerius Gratus, Pilate's predecessor, had tactfully issued coins harmlessly adorned with palm branches or ears of corn, familiar enough Jewish symbols, but as early as A.D. 29 Pilate issued copper coins bearing the *lituus* or pagan priest's staff, a symbol of the imperial cult which was bound to be obnoxious to the people. It was calculated provocation, and comparatively safe, because the users were insulted individually, and the coinage did not produce collective demonstrations of hostility. Pilate too felt safe since, in the tribute-money, the Jews were compromising over an idolatrous symbol, the emperor's own portrait. Each man swallowed the new piece of arrogance and said nothing. Seianus fell in A.D. 31 and, significantly enough, the issue of such provocative coins ceased about this time.

THIS COIN ISSUED BY PONTIUS PILATE *bears the lituus, or pagan priest's staff.*

Coins, therefore, and they are part of the stuff of archaeology, reveal something of the foolish and distracted man who sent Christ to the cross. It was clearly the Pilate of the offensive coins who stung his enemies with the inscription over the cross, and returned the savage answer: "What I have written, I have written."

Pilate at Caesarea

There are two brief footnotes to the story of Pilate which archaeology can add. The first is from Caesarea, and is as recent as 1961. A slab of stone from the Roman theater there bears Pontius Pilate's name, fragmented and half-obliterated, but obviously his, and without accompanying titles or explanation. With the remnant of Pilate's name there are the letters . . . IBERIEVM. Was the theater near a temple to Tiberius (a 'Tiberieum') built by Pilate, so eager to be, as the Jews sneered, "friend of Caesar"? Perhaps the continued excavation of the important site will produce more. The Israelis are busy at the task. Archaeology has a long chapter to write on those extensive ruins.

Caesarea lies on the open coast of Palestine. It is a rough and harborless littoral, low sandhills swept by the sea winds and the Mediterranean surf. The coast is strewn with ancient harbor works, where engineers have striven to provide a haven for ships. The sea has won in every case, and the endless assault of the waves has broken down and swallowed mole and breakwater all the way up the old Philistine coast to the jutting promontory of Carmel, which provides Haifa with a modicum of shelter from the southwest winds.

At Caesarea the Mediterranean surge had its hardest task. Herod the First spent twelve years, from 25 to 13 B.C., building his great port there. It was a matter of life and death for him to give the Romans a safe bridgehead. His subtle diplomacy aimed at serving Augustus, whose eastern legions, after all, kept him in power, and simultaneously conciliating the Jews, his restless and resentful subjects. Hence the apparent contradiction of a temple to Augustus, the perron of which can still be seen at Samaria, and a temple to Jehovah in Jerusalem. It is a testimony to Herod's ruthless ability that he carried through this dual policy and, in the end, died in his bed.

Caesarea gave the Romans an entry and a base. The sea wall was a notable triumph of engineering. How the blocks

THE RUINS OF CAESAREA, *where Herod built a great port. This city served as a Roman base and administrative center.*

of limestone, some of them fifty feet long, were put in place to form the mole, itself some two hundred feet wide and standing in twenty fathoms of water, is not known. It would tax all the resources of a highly mechanized society. The sea wall curved around to form a haven. Behind it, on the low sandy shore, a semicircle of wall protected the town, its houses, racecourse, theater and temples.

Nothing of Herod's harbor is visible from the boulder-strewn shore today, although the dry dock for the galleys may still be traced. The theater with its high curve of seats is prominent. It is there that Pilate for some reason set up his inscription. It was discovered by Professor Antonio Frova, the Italian archaeologist.

There are sundry Roman foundations on the crowded site. Somewhere among those stones Philip had his house, Cornelius his barrack-room, and Paul his cell. Crusader ruins dominate the scene, for the Frankish invaders saw the advantage of Caesarea as a beachhead, as clearly as did Herod and his Roman masters. North of the town is a fragment of a vast aqueduct which brought in water from some distant spring, and must have been the fortress' most vulnerable link. Surely somewhere the archaeologists must find vast storage tanks. Water would be a problem for the garrison even with uninterrupted command of the sea lanes. Pilate built an aqueduct into Jerusalem, as we have seen, and built it with the forbidden temple funds. It would be interesting to know whether he gave such thought to the headquarters town.

Pilate at Jerusalem

The second footnote to the story is the result of the painstaking work of the Dominican archaeologists under the Antonia Tower, the headquarters of the governor in Jerusalem. It appears that, deep in the crypt, the Pavement where Pilate sat to judge Christ may be seen. It is always to be remembered that the streets of the city today follow the ancient lines, though indeed they may be twenty feet higher than the levels of the first century, but W. F. Albright, whose authority is beyond question, is sure that the pavement is Roman. There is a section of pathway scored to give grip to the horses' hooves. It is separated from the rest of the pavement by a row of holes for posts. There are deep funnels to drain away the rain water. Further back, in the floor of a common hall, there are incisions in the stones where the soldiers played their games. One pattern might have been for a kind of chess, or perhaps for noughts and crosses. It is infinitely pathetic to see such marks of human frivolity in the very place where the drama of Eternity was moving to its climax.

ARCHAEOLOGY AND THE
RESURRECTION OF CHRIST

CHAPTER 6

ARCHAEOLOGY AND THE RESURRECTION OF CHRIST

ON THE RESURRECTION, ARCHAEOLOGY HAS A PIECE OF astonishing evidence to offer, for it is quite beyond question that one of the most interesting archaeological discoveries in Palestine during the century of exploration its ancient sites have seen, is a simple slab of white marble from Nazareth, the hometown of Christ. The stone found its way in 1878 into the collection of a distinguished antiquarian named Froehner, who noted it down in his catalog simply thus: "Slab of marble sent from Nazareth in 1878."

The Nazareth Decree

Froehner was an eccentric person, but an archaeologist of exact scholarship and distinction, most unlikely to have been deceived. If he so recorded the origin of the Nazareth stone, the statement can be quite unreservedly accepted. As a collector, on the other hand, Froehner guarded his treasures jealously, and derived a perverse and lamentable enjoyment from the possession of antiquities of which the world of scholarship knew nothing. Publication, to

75

Froehner's mind, diminished his personal interest in possession.

In the order of nature Froehner passed away, and the items of his fine collection found their way to the French treasure house of the Louvre. The piece of marble from Nazareth was housed in the Cabinet de Medailles, and at long last, in 1930 in fact, over half a century after its arrival in Europe, Michel Rostovtzeff, the great historian, cast his eye on its rather irregular lines of clear Greek script. He stared in astonishment, for here was an inscription of unique importance unknown to scholarship.

This is what he read:

Ordinance of Caesar. It is my pleasure that graves and tombs remain undisturbed in perpetuity for those who have made them for the cult of their ancestors, or children, or members of their house. If, however, any man lay information that another has either demolished them, or has in any other way extracted the buried, or has maliciously transferred them to other places in order to wrong them, or has displaced the sealing or other stones, against such a one I order that a trial be instituted, as in respect of the gods, so in regard to the cult of mortals. For it shall be much more obligatory to honor the buried. Let it be absolutely forbidden for anyone to disturb them. In the case of contravention I desire that the offender be sentenced to capital punishment on charge of violation of sepulture.

Need one stress the significance of a decree concerning moving the stone coverings of tombs, and extracting the bodies of the dead, which comes from the town where Christ lived? The scholars were not slow to move, and the Abbe Cumont, Rostovtzeff's friend, and a first-rate ancient historian, was quickly in the field with an account of the inscription, an attempt to date it, an analysis of the language, and an account of its significance.

Since the Abbe Cumont's article, which appeared in the *Journal of Hellenic Studies* in 1932, the field has become a well-trodden one, and it is a fact that every Roman em-

THE NAZARETH INSCRIPTION,
issued by Claudius Caesar
and cut on a slab of white
marble, is the first re-
corded imperial response to
Christianity.

peror, from Augustus to Hadrian, with the exception of
Caligula, has been named as the author or promulgator of the
Nazareth Decree. No overwhelming reason, however, has
been put forward for abandoning a position originally taken
by Arnaldo Monigliano, the brilliant Italian historian, who
thought the decree a rescript of Claudius.

But before considering the evidence for the dating which
seems to be reasonable, let us look at a few other points
which thirty years of live discussion and controversy have
more or less established. First of all the Greek is a rather
poor translation of a Latin original. As with schoolboy ex-
ercises, the Latin idiom peeps a little clumsily through the
Greek translation. The decree therefore came to Palestine in
Latin, and was done into Greek for the perusal of the
bilingual inhabitants of Nazareth by some secretary of the
Governor.

The Nazareth Decree — a Rescript

We have called the inscription so far a *decree*. But should
we do so in all exactitude? Perhaps not. Edicts and decrees
of the imperial government tended to find expression in
rather more elegant language and less blunt terminology than
the inscription quoted above. Difficulties of this sort dis-
appear if the inscription is assumed to be a reply, a rescript,
to use the technical expression, of the emperor, addressed to
the local governor, the legate of Syria or the procurator of
Judaea, who had addressed to him a question on a specific
case of tomb-robbery. The final volume of Pliny's correspondence contains many replies of this sort from the pen
of the Emperor Trajan, outlining in conversational rather
than official style the ruler's will on some matter in question.
One of these rescripts is, as we have seen, famous for the first
outline which it gives of imperial policy in the matter of the
rising Christian Church. Indeed, included also in this volume
of quite invaluable letters and replies, is one in which the
governor of Bithynia makes inquiry regarding the moving of

the remains of the dead, and another which contains the emperor's written judgment.

Pliny writes:

> Having been petitioned by some persons to grant them the liberty of removing the relics of their deceased relations on the grounds that their tombs were destroyed by age, or broken down by the invasion of flood waters, I thought proper, Sir, knowing that it is usual at Rome to consult the College of Pontiffs on such matters, to ask you, as head of that sacred order, what course you would have me follow.

Trajan replies briefly, and one imagines a little testily, for Pliny was a most assiduous correspondent. He writes:

> The obligation to petition the pontifical college is a hardship for the provincials, when they have just reasons for removing the ashes of their ancestors. It will be better, therefore, for you to follow the example of your predecessors, and grant or deny this liberty as you see reasonable.

There, then, is a perfect example of a question and a rescript. If the Nazareth document is a rescript, it must have come to Palestine in reply to an official request for instructions regarding the opening of tombs, and it does seem curious that the stone should have been set up at Nazareth and only at Nazareth, the town from which Christ came, He whose empty tomb had given the Christian Church its Gospel. And why was the emperor, whichever emperor it was, stirred to such drastic threatenings? Capital punishment for the less heinous crimes was not a common feature of Roman law until the third century, when the lengthening shadows of social and legal decadence lay heavily across the Empire. What sort of question, or what flagrant abuse, moved a Roman ruler, steeped in the legal tradition of his race, to depart so notably from general practice, and to lay down such harsh provision in one part only of the Empire, and that part the Palestinian town of Jesus of Nazareth?

Dating the Rescript

Two converging lines of evidence suggest that the inscription falls within the decade which closed with A.D. 50. The style and execution of the lettering satisfy the practiced epigraphist that the work belongs to the first half of that century. And then, and this rules out three emperors, Augustus, Tiberius and Caligula, the central Roman government did not take over the administration of Galilee until the death of its puppet king Agrippa in A.D. 44. No decree could have been set up in Nazareth by the governor of Syria or the procurator of Judaea before that date. The autonomy of the area may have been a legal fiction, but the Romans, of all imperialists, knew the value of legal fictions. Consider, too, the incident at the trial of Christ: "And they were the more fierce saying, 'He stirreth up the people teaching throughout all Jewry, beginning from Galilee to this place.' When Pilate heard of Galilee he asked whether the man were a Galilean. And as soon as he knew that he belonged to Herod's jurisdiction, he sent him to Herod . . ." (Matt. 23:5-7). No Roman authority would presume to set up inscribed laws at Nazareth before A.D. 44, and if we can rely upon the epigraphical conclusion that A.D. 50 is approaching near to the latest date for work so styled and executed, it becomes possible to hazard a guess about the emperor who sent the reply to Palestine.

It could have been none other than Claudius. And once we accept that statement, one or two points of confirmation immediately appear. Claudius was an odd person, a sort of Roman James the First, who would have been much happier with his books than with officers of State. Ancient historians persisted in calling him mad, but the more Claudius' actual achievements are studied, the clearer becomes the impression that he was a man of learning and of no mean ability. He was probably a spastic, or the victim of some other form of cerebral disturbance, whose faulty coordinations conveyed an unjust impression of subnormality, and resulted, in his early years, in ridicule and misunderstanding which damaged his personality. It is clear that, anxious to carry on the religious reforms of Augustus, he was deeply informed about, and genuinely interested in, the religious situation in the Mediterranean world.

THIS TOMB WITH A ROLLING STONE *for closing its entrance is still in operating condition. The tomb was found on the back slopes of the Mount of Olives, near Bethphage.*

A long letter, for example, has survived in which Claudius seeks to regulate the serious Jewish problem of Alexandria. This letter, certainly a rescript, and a document of great historical and constitutional importance, was found among the papyri in 1920, and appears to contain the first secular reference to Christian missionaries. It was written in A.D. 41, and expressly forbids the Alexandrian Jews "to bring or invite other Jews to come by sea from Syria. If they do not abstain from this conduct," Claudius threatens, "I shall proceed against them for fomenting a malady common to the world."

Note the language. It is the rather downright style of the Nazareth inscription, and the language of a man who had studied the Jewish religious problem, and found it irritating. It would be surprising if Claudius, with these preoccupations, was not the first Roman outside Palestine to hear of the Christians.

Christ and Claudius

Historians are definitely of this opinion. The Acts of the Apostles (18:2), confirmed by two Roman historians, Orosius and Suetonius, says that Claudius expelled the Jews from Rome. This was in A.D. 49, and note how the date coincides with the likely one for the Nazareth Inscription. Suetonius adds that Claudius acted thus because of rioting in the ghetto *"at the instigation of one Chrestos."*[1]

The reference is obviously to Christ, and as Arnaldo Momigliano once insisted,[2] those who deny that Suetonius made the simple mistake of confusing two Greek words, *"christos"* and *"chrestos,"* must undertake the difficult task of proving their contention. To suppose that the Roman biographer was referring to Christ is undoubtedly more reasonable than any other suggestion.

The situation may, therefore, with much probability be thus reconstructed. In the forties of the first century the first Christian preaching was heard in Rome, and the synagogue was in bitter opposition. Trouble in the Jewish quarter and a wave of arrests appeal to a dual interest in the Emperor, to his curiosity over religion and his awareness of the Jewish problem, as well as to his predilection for the bench. He hears the case, and it proves a strange story. The trouble, he gathers, is about one named Christ, who, his followers aver, "rose from the dead." The defense of the rabbis is obviously the Pharisaic version of the empty tomb as reported by Matthew: "His disciples came and stole away the body" (28:13).

There is a quite authentic touch of Claudius' well-documented whimsicality and carefulness in the result. Unable to decide the issue, he banished all Jews. He must then

1 *Claudius* 25:4.
2 *Claudius the Emperor and His Achievements* (1962).

have made inquiries in Palestine, and heard from the authorities that the preaching of the Gospel of the Resurrection was rife. "What shall I do?" asks the governor. Back comes the rescript. "Quench the trouble at its place of origin by a stern decree." Or, if the Inscription is not a rescript, it could be a quotation from one of Claudius' long letters on religious problems, dutifully set up by the local authorities. If this reasoning is sound three facts emerge. The first is that Christian preaching began in Rome much earlier than was once supposed, and many years before the arrival of Paul. The second fact is that imperial action against the Church must have begun with Claudius, and not with Nero after the Great Fire in A.D. 64. Finally it would appear that, in Rome, as in Jerusalem, the stark fact of the empty tomb was accepted by the foes of Christ. And so, in the words of an emperor, the twentieth century reads the first secular comment on the Easter story, and what is virtually legal testimony to its central fact.

The Metaphorical Reference to Resurrection

The theme of resurrection appeared metaphorically in the teaching of Christ. "Truly, I tell you," He said, "except a corn of wheat fall into the ground and die, it remains alone; but if it die it brings forth much fruit" (John 12:24). Curiously enough, the figure was part of the Eleusinian cult of Demeter the Earth Goddess. This "mystery religion" was domiciled at the great temple along the coast near Athens, and many thousands of Athenians were initiated into it every year. "Mystery" cults had their origin in fertility rituals and Nature-worship, and played a very large part in Greek religious experience. They owed their name to the fact that many of their rites were private, involving information withheld from all but the initiated. They tended to degenerate into the sexuality which surrounded such cults as those of Artemis at Ephesus, and Aphrodite at Corinth, but some of them developed the elements of true worship, and through

ELEUSIS, NEAR ATHENS, *includes the site of the Temple of Demeter (foreground, top photo). Among the sculptured fragments from the temple (right) is a bundle of wheat.*

their teaching, ceremonies, and sacraments, gave birth and stimulus to genuine spiritual experience. Their theological language and practice was not without its influence on the vocabulary of the New Testament, and the organization of Christian worship.

There seems no doubt that the Eleusinian "mysteries" were of a pure order, and played a beneficent part in Athenian life. The annual ceremonies were elaborate, and aimed both at stirring deep emotions, and promoting a conviction of spiritual rebirth. Little, of coure, is known of them, in the very nature of the case. Initiates kept their vows of secrecy. But it is known that part of the ceremonial was the uplifting of an ear of corn, which, in the symbolism of the cult, was meant to signify death and rebirth.

Eleusis is now an industrial suburb of Athens. The ruins of the sacred precincts are sadly shattered, and perhaps not tended with the care which the Greeks usually bestow upon their antiquities. But beside the path to the Great Hall lies a broken frieze, and one of its carved emblems is a sheaf of corn.

Perhaps it is fanciful to see any link between the Great Athenian mystery cult and the words of Christ about a corn of wheat. But it is odd that the remark should have been made in the context in which John reports it . . . "And there were certain Greeks among those that came up to worship at the festival, and they came to Philip and requested him, saying, Sir we would see Jesus . . . ." The visitors were probably converts to Judaism from the Greek colonies of the Decapolis. Was Christ speaking in words they might be supposed to understand?

Early Christianity in China

A second footnote to the story of the resurrection, and a facet of its archaeology, comes, oddly enough, from ancient China. It is a story worth telling in view of the curious philosophies of a modern Gnosticism which seek today to "demythologize" the central story of the faith.

In Sianfu, in 1625, an inscribed stone was found which had lain buried for nine centuries. Workmen digging foundation trenches came upon a large monument, over seven feet high and three feet wide. It had been set up in A.D. 781, and contained a statement of Christian belief, and a description of the arrival, in A.D. 635, at Sianfu, then a capital of the Tang dynasty, of a missionary from Tutsin, or Syria, named Olopan. There was also an account of the fortunes of the church which he founded, and a few other relevant details in verse and prose.

It was a document of early Christianity in China, and undoubtedly genuine. Edward Gibbon, whose sceptical and penetrating mind left nothing unexamined, accepted the evidence without hesitation. In the forty-seventh chapter of his famous *Decline and Fall of the Roman Empire,* Gibbon describes the scattering abroad by homeland persecution of the followers of the fifth-century Syrian bishop, Nestorius. They fled east to Socotra, to Ceylon, to India — and to China. "In their progress by sea and land," writes Gibbon, "the Nestorians entered China by the port of Canton and the northern residence of Sigan." This was Sianfu.

They found persecution again. Gibbon continues: "The mandarins, who affect in public the reason of philosophers, are devoted in private to every form of popular superstition. They cherished and they confounded the gods of Palestine and of India; but the propagation of Christianity awakened the jealousy of the State, and after a short vicissitude of favor and oblivion, the foreign sect expired." Then Gibbon adds a footnote: "The Christianity of China, between the seventh and tenth centuries, is invincibly proved by the consent of Chinese, Arabian, Syrian and Latin evidence. The inscription of Sianfu which describes the fortunes of the Nestorian Church is accused of forgery by La Croze, Voltaire and others, who become the dupes of their own cunning while they are afraid of a Jesuistical fraud."

The forgery charge survived until Renan, but the Nestorian Monument is now accepted as a genuine document. But why did the matter suggest more modern heresies? It was simply the reflection that the attempt to recast basic Christian doctrine in the terminology of an ephemeral philosophy, the current vice among theologians, has led to the collapse of the Church on earlier occasions. To recast is precisely what the Nestorian missionaries in China sought to do, and no exception can be taken to an effort to preach a vital message in language which the immediate audience will understand, and in "thought-forms," if that word means anything, proper to the habits of their minds. This is beyond all dispute the way to preach persuasively.

But, and here is the rub, the content of the preaching must not, in the same act, be eroded, attenuated or lost. One can search in vain through the mystical and highly philosophical language of the Nestorian inscription for a clear statement of the two central doctrines of the New Testament, the atoning death of Christ, and the resurrection which was its confirmation. The ethical content is there, and the return of the Saviour to Heaven, but the rest is gone.

Why? Over the century and a half since the coming of the first valiant missionaries, the Chinese Church had won a measure of favor in high imperial circles, but was also aware of the suspicion and dislike of the philosophically-minded, educated classes. Rightly, the Christians went to great lengths to find points of contact, to bridge the gap between the doctrines they had to teach, and the thought and language of those whom they sought to influence. And, as so often happens in such contexts, they went too far, and lost the real content of their message, just as the rationalist theologians of today have done in their encounter with existentialism.

The result? The Church died. It was dry rot, not persecution, suicide nor murder, which ensured its demise. Or at least its passing as a church. The Japanese scholar, P. V. Saeki, who has studied the Nestorian inscription intensively, believes that the Nestorian Church still exists in two forms. The twenty million Moslems of China contain a host of its descendants. They had been left with only a vague monotheism, and such a union was easy — ecumenism with a vengeance. Others are the secret society followers of the "Religion of the Pill of Immortality," which seems to contain in creed and ritual, some vestigial memories of Christianity. History is dismally repetitive.

From Aswan, Egypt

A third footnote comes from Egypt. The archaeologists have been racing the water in the Nile Valley. Nasser's high dam at Aswan is to submerge every 250 miles of it, and the great statues of Ramses II, on which so much engineering wit is expended, are not the only treasures threatened by the flood.

There are remains much more fragile, and the digging teams are working hard to rescue their treasures from the water. The most recent discovery fell to archaeologists of Chicago University. In the remains of a tenth-century Christian monastery on the Egyptian-Sudanese border, they found an ancient Coptic prayer book. It contained a hymn to the cross, attributed to Jesus on the eve of the Crucifixion, together with an imaginary conversation between Jesus and His disciples after the resurrection.

The hymn was allegedly composed on the Mount of Olives, the long ridge south of Jerusalem, with the magnificent view of the Holy City tilted like a great platter on the further slope. The mystical words of the opening verse run:

> *Rise up, rise up, O holy Cross*
> *and lift me, O Cross,*
> *I shall mount upon you, O Cross,*

> *They shall hang me upon you*
> *as a witness to them.*

Are the words authentic? It is clear enough from the
records of the four gospels that Jesus foresaw and foretold
His death. It was obvious enough that the corrupt and
collaborating authorities of Judaism would not let Him live.
Once grant that the collision was inevitable, and the ghastly
manner of the end could also be foreseen. He would be
handed over to the Romans, and the Romans would crucify
Him. "A cross" was also a symbol for a grievous load. "Let
him take up his cross daily and follow me," was a saying
which has supplied all the languages of Christendom with a
figure of speech.

Grant all this, and it still remains difficult to believe that
Christ uttered the words of the hymn. They are a reading
back into the events of the Passion week of a later Christian
theology, and the hymn is no doubt based on one of the
many apocryphal accounts which has not survived. It is all
so alien to the poignant simplicity of the narrative in the
New Testament.

The story of the conversation after the resurrection has
the same faint air of unreality. Four days before the Ascen-
sion, and on the same Mount of Olives, the story runs, Jesus
was asked by Peter to "reveal a mystery" to them. Note first
those words. They contain a flavor of Paul's use of the word
"mystery," but are in no way similar to anything else said by
the apostle . . . Christ answered: "O my chosen one, Peter,
and you my fellow heirs, I have not hidden anything from
you ever concerning which you have enquired of me, nor
shall I hide anything from you now. Ask me anything which
you wish to know."

Whereupon Peter asked the Master to unfold "the mystery
of the cross," and tell why Christ will carry the cross at the
Last Judgment: "O my chosen one, Peter, and you my
brethren," Christ answered, "you are aware of the lies which

were told against me on the cross, and the spitting at me, and the words of contempt uttered against me. This is why I shall bring the cross with me, to reveal their shame, and put their sin upon their heads."

No attentive reader of the gospels can fail to mark the difference, but the story is worth quoting to show, in contrast, the strength and simple power of the gospel narratives. The monastery text from the floor of the future Aswan lake, shows what the tampering of time can do to an authentic narrative. Here, if they will, is material on which the "form critics" may exercise their perverse ingenuity. Let them spare the brief, clear narratives of the Risen Christ.

ARCHAEOLOGY AND THE
ACTS OF THE APOSTLES

CHAPTER 7

ARCHAEOLOGY AND THE ACTS OF THE APOSTLES

Any good library of New Testament literature contains a dozen sturdy volumes on Luke, Paul, and the Church of Asia Minor from the pen of William Mitchell Ramsay, classical scholar, archaeologist, and historian, to whose work we have already made brief reference. The archaeology of the Acts of the Apostles is bound intimately with the record of Sir William's life and career, and many who are well acquainted with his writings are unaware of the romance of the personal experience which lies behind them.

The Recovery of Luke the Historian

Speaking on one occasion in reminiscent mood before the students of the Moody Bible Institute in Chicago, the great New Testament scholar told how he had planned his life far otherwise. For the young classicist who sought a life of learning in Victoria's England, the path was hedged and straight. It led from the student's bench in mellow and ancient colleges through scholarship and fellowship to the dons' table and the professor's chair. From such a course, early in his life, Ramsay was deflected by illness and misfortune. There is something Pauline in the story of events which followed. In his humble testimony in Chicago Sir William told how, though he knew little more faith than that which consisted in a hunger for truth and God, circumstances, with seeming compulsion, headed him in the direction of Asia Minor.

In strange and unexpected fashion provision and opportunity brought the worker to his task, but in many ways he was still curiously unfitted to undertake it. It was the heyday of that destructive criticism which began in the universities of Germany and inspired, the world over, that revulsion from biblical Christianity for which this century has paid dearly. The breakdown of German Christianity, and the vast weakness of a still convalescent Christendom before dynamic evil, are two visible results of the reckless scholarship which began with Wellhausen, and left no tradition unassailed.

Ramsay, the future champion of Luke and Paul, accepted with little question the popular contemporary verdict that the Acts of the Apostles was a late second century piece of imaginative reconstruction. The young scholar indeed had no intention of spending the three years available under his research grant in anything so trivial as the discredited records of New Testament romancing.

It was the compulsion of fact, at work upon an honest mind, which brought about the change. Acts 14:6 states: "They . . . . fled into Lystra and Derbe, cities of Lycaonia . . . ." In other words, in passing from Iconium to Lystra, one crossed the frontier. Most geographers, basing their contention on what appeared to be competent ancient authority, dismissed the Lucan statement as a mistake. Local inscriptions, obviously more trustworthy than ancient or modern geographers, convinced Ramsay that the writer of Acts was correct. The frontier of Lycaonia lay where he said it did.

NEAR THE CITY OF KONYA *(modern Iconium) is this thresh-ing floor typical of the Lycaonian plain. With a continuing history from the days of Paul, Konya is still a prominent trading center.*

Ramsay may be left to tell the story in his own words. "I may fairly claim," he wrote in 1898, "to have entered on this investigation without prejudice in favor of the conclusion which I shall now seek to justify to the reader. On the contrary, I began with a mind unfavorable to it, for the ingenuity and apparent completeness of the Tubingen theory had at one time quite convinced me. It did not then lie in my line of life to investigate the subject minutely; but more recently I found myself brought in contact with the Book of Acts as an authority for the topography, antiquities and society of Asia Minor. It was gradually borne in upon me that in various details the narrative showed marvelous truth. In fact, beginning with a fixed idea that the word was essenti-ally came to find it a useful ally in some obscure and difficult evidence as trustworthy for first-century conditions, I gradu-ally came to find it a useful ally in some obscure and difficult investigations." The whole of the chapter is worth reading. Historical criticism has obviously traveled far from the days when F. C. Bauer could speak of statements in Acts as "intentional deviations from historical truth."[1]

It might in passing be noted that A. N. Sherwin-White, the Oxford classicist and historian, has similarly written enthusiastic pages on the theme.[2] He stresses the exactitude of the historical framework, the precision of detail of time and place, the feel and tone of provincial city life, through the eyes of an alert Hellenistic Jew. "Acts," he writes, "takes us on a conducted tour of the Greek and Roman world with detail and narrative so interwoven as to be inseparable."

Such was the beginning of a long process of delighted discovery which convinced Ramsay that, in Luke the historian, he was dealing with one of the great writers of Greece. For accuracy of detail, and for evocation of atmosphere, Luke stands, in fact, with Thucydides. The Acts of the Apostles is no shoddy product of pious imagining, but a trustworthy record of great events. And it was the spadework of archaeology which first revealed the truth.

The Demonstration of Lucan Accuracy

Very many illustrations might be culled from the story of Ramsay's work. For example, in the same Lystra to which Paul escaped from Iconium, Ramsay found a native inscription dedicating a statue to Zeus and Hermes. The two deities were evidently linked in the local cult. These twain, it will be remembered, Latinized in the Authorized Version as Jupiter and Mercury, were the gods to whom the enthusiastic Lycaonians likened Paul and Barnabas. The accuracy of the background is striking.

Luke's meticulous care for the correct designation and definition is again and again apparent. When Paul crossed from Asia into Europe, Luke, his chronicler, on bringing the

[1] W. M. Ramsay. *St. Paul the Traveller and Roman Citizen* [London, 1898] pp. 7, 8.

[2] A. N. Sherwin-White; *Roman Society and Roman Law in the New Testament* [Oxford, 1963].

story to Philippi, described the town as "the first of the district." Even Hort marked this as a mistake, since the Greek word *meris* appeared never to be used for "region." The Egyptian papyri, however, revealed that Luke's Greek was better than that of his scholarly editor. The word, it was obvious, was quite commonly used for "district" in the first century, and especially in Macedonia.

But another difficulty remained. It has been demonstrated with some likelihood that Luke came from Philippi. Had enthusiasm for his hometown led the physician astray, for was not Amphipolis the local capital? Loyalty did play a part, and the amiable foible is a clear mark of Lucan authenticity. But there was no distortion of fact. "Afterwards," writes Ramsay,[3] "Philippi quite outstripped its rival; but it was at that time in such a position that Amphipolis was ranked first by general consent, Philippi first by its own consent. These cases of rivalry between two or even three cities for the dignity and title of 'first' are familiar to every student of the history of the Greek cities; and though no other evidence is known to show that Philippi had as yet begun to claim the title, yet this single passage is conclusive. The descriptive phrase is like a lightning flash in the darkness of local history, revealing in startling clearness the whole situation to those whose eyes are trained to catch the character of Greek city-history. . . ." It is odd to see the personality of the historian peep out. And what, in the light of it, of the rash theory of second-century romancing?

Luke also calls the local officials of Philippi "praetors." The term seemed incorrect until inscriptions established the fact that the title was a courtesy one for the magistrates of the Roman colony; and as usual Luke uses the term commonly employed in educated circles.

Thessalonica provides another chastening example. In Acts 17:6, 8, Luke twice calls the "rulers" of the city "politarchs." Since the term was unknown elsewhere, the

[3] *St. Paul the Traveller and Roman Citizen*, pp. 206, 207.

THE RUINS OF PHILIPPI *with a general view of the forum (above) looking west, and a close-up of an ornamented capital of the basilica (below).*

IN THE HEART OF SALONIKA *(modern Thessalonica), Galerius' Arch, located on the Egnation Way, displays the well-preserved detail of its ancient relief.*

omniscient critics of the historian dismissed the word as yet another mistake. Today it is to be read high and clear in an arch spanning a street of modern Salonika, and sixteen other examples occur. A similar story of vindication could be told of the title "protos," applied in Acts 28:7 to the governor of Malta.

The "South Galatian Theory"

One of Ramsay's major historical theories remains to be examined, for the evidence on which it was based is largely archaeological. One should rather say epigraphical, for, as we have already illustrated, it is the mute and solid evidence of the ancient inscription which has played so large a part in the establishment of Luke's historical reputation. Epigraphy was the main source of the "south Galatian theory."

Phrygia was an ancient country of Asia Minor noted in legend and history. It was immensely rich, for it straddled the ancient trade routes, and its civilization was early and precocious. In Roman times the area was comprehended in the provinces of Asia and Galatia. Of the latter province the northern portion was wild and uncivilized, and populated largely by descendants of the Gallo-Celtic tribesmen who had broken into Asia Minor in an old tribal migration, and had given Galatia its name. The southern portion was civilized and sophisticated, and included such great cities as Iconium and Antioch.

It was perversely assumed that Paul's Galatian churches were in the north. The assumption was based on numerous vague notions — that southern Galatia was Greek not Phrygian, that the instability of the Galatian church was a fruit of Celtic headiness, and so forth. The careful collection of epigraphical evidence proved again that Luke's geographical terminology (for example in Acts 16:6) could not be, as Ramsay phrases it, "more precise, definite, and clear."

One inscription speaks of the "Phrygian" Antioch, and others have made it quite obvious that the administrative district of South Galatia was Phrygian in language and tradition. There was, moreover, an uprooted minority of Jews whose presence accounts for the Judaistic tendencies in the church. It is clear, too, on epigraphical as well as historical evidence, that the whole area saw one of the earliest triumphs of Christian evangelism. There is an enormous corpus of Christian inscriptions from the area. And when one remembers that the Crusaders marched through Asia Minor to Palestine without leaving one written memorial, the literacy of the Asian Christians is emphasized.

Ramsay's demonstration that Galatia in the Acts of the Apostles was South Galatia has quite solved the difficulties which beset those who regarded the book as an unreliable fabrication of late origin. On the contrary, it stands proven that the Galatian passages in the book could only have been written by a first-century historian who spoke naturally in the geographical terminology of contemporary inscriptions.

Further Touchstones for the Acts

This brief account of the archaeological contribution to the understanding of the Acts of the Apostles has naturally omitted much. It is amazing that so much historical material has survived time's "wreckful siege." One would not expect, for example, in a region so trampled by the destructiveness of men, clear evidence of the family of Sergius Paulus. Yet two inscriptions appear to refer to a son and a daughter of the Roman governor of Cyprus. And from the ruins of Ephesus, who would have expected the carved name of Demetrius to emerge? It cannot be proved that "Demetrius, son of Menophilus, son of Tryphon of the Thousand Boreis" was, in fact, the persecutor of Paul, but Hicks has made, in Ramsay's view, a strong case for the identification.

Archaeological discovery relevant to Luke's vivid story, his "conducted tour" of the cities of the Eastern Mediterranean world, is difficult to marshall. Shall we turn the pages rapidly and touch here and there an illustrative detail? Ephesus, from which the Demetrius inscription has emerged, has much to offer the traveler in the steps of Paul, most of which may be more conveniently dealt with when the Apocalypse brings us back to the great Asian city as it appeared a generation later. The frequent appearance of the "Asiarchs" in Ephesian inscriptions may be mentioned here. These "rulers of Asia," who were prompt to protect Paul during the unpleasant riot, were the honorary custodians of the imperial cult, soon to be, in that very province, the bitter persecutors of Christianity, but at this time not unwilling to see a kind of ally in the religion which was harming the great fertility cult of Artemis.

For some other inscriptions turn back to the story of Corinth. . . . The road winds down from Athens and over the deep trench of the Corinth canal, a project dreamed of by Nero, and actually begun and abandoned during the emperor's stay in Greece. The proud praetorian guards, who were employed on the task, doubtless proved a difficult labor force. The road ascends as it moves south, and the apricot roofs of modern Corinth come into view, with the Corinthian Gulf running into the mauve distance to the west, and the blue Saronic Gulf to the east. In late summer there is the heavy smell of drying currants in the air, and the visitor remembers that the word "currant" derives from Corinth. And Corinth, like all the other place names ending in -inth, like the words "plinth" and "labyrinth," are words from the unknown tongue spoken in the Aegean before the Greeks came.

THE TEMPLE OF APOLLO, *in Corinth, was constructed in the middle of the fifth century* B.C.

Further south, under the great precipitous outcrop of the Acrocorinthus, lies all that is left of old Corinth, once the cosmopolitan crossroads of the middle Mediterranean. In the great days of Greek independence, and intercity strife, Corinth had been a naval power to challenge Athens. When Roman imperialism spread eastwards, and Achaea became a province, the port inevitably became a nodal point of communications, and a busy center of trade. The dragway by which the ships were hauled over the isthmus is still traceable.

Corinth was at strife with Rome in 146 B.C., and was destroyed in one of the most ruthless acts of vandalism in Roman history. Of the Corinth which thus fell, only seven Doric columns of the temple of Apollo, spared by the superstitious demolition squads, remain standing, high and prominent above the market place of the later town. When Paul reminded the Corinthians that they were "the temples of the Holy Spirit," it would inevitably be this ruin which would rise to the mind's eye, windswept, clean, prominent for all to see.

Almost exactly a century after Corinth was beaten thus to the ground, Julius Caesar restored it under a wide colonization scheme which, but for the senseless act of his assassination, might have had salutary possibilities in the Mediterranean world. It was Caesar's Corinth which Paul visited almost a century later still, and where, in the midst of the polyglot and cosmopolitan population of a notoriously vicious port, he founded the most troublesome and difficult of his Christian communities. It is also Caesar's Corinth on which the archaeologists have worked so busily, uncovering the agora, or market place, and part of the two roads which run down to Lechaeum, the port on the Corinthian Gulf, and Cenchrea, the twin landing place on the Aegean side of the isthmus. On the Lechaeum road a fragmentary inscription marks the synagogue of the Jews, where Paul preached. Across one end of the excavated market place runs a stone platform, six to seven feet high, and faced with marble. It is the *bema* where Gallio, Seneca's brother, sat to hear the case of Paul. His governorship incidentally, is dated A.D. 52 by an inscription at Delphi. A tantalizing block of marble found near the theater, bears another fragmentary inscription which reads: "Erastus, for the office of aedile, laid this pavement at his own expense." Is this Erastus, the city treasurer, who was a foundation member of the Corinthian church?

Turn on to Chapter 20 and the story of the boy Eutychus, who, overcome by the fumes of the oil lamps, and perhaps no less by Paul's monumental sermon, fell from a high window. No proof is needed that fallible mortals can fall asleep during the best of sermons, nor, indeed, that a fall from a high window ledge can have tragic results, but it is curiously interesting to find a second-century papyrus containing a report of just such an accident. It runs:

Hierax, strategus of the Oxyrhynchite nome, to Claudius Serenus, assistant. A copy of the application which has been presented to me by Leonidas is herewith sent to you, in order that you may take a public physician and inspect the dead body referred to and after delivering it over for burial make with him a report in writing. Signed by me. The 23rd year of Marcus Aurelius Commodus Antoninus Caesar the lord, Hathur 7.

To Hierax, strategus, from Leonidas, having Tauris for mother, of Senepta. At a late hour of yesterday the sixth, while a festival was taking place at Senepta and castanet-dancers were giving the customary performance at the house of Plution my son-in-law . . . his slave Epaphroditus, aged about 8 years, wishing to lean out from the house-top of the said house to see the castanet-dancers, fell to his death. I therefore present this application and request you, if it please you, to appoint one of your assistants to come to Senepta, in order that the body of Epaphroditus may receive the necessary burial. The 23rd year of the Emperor Caesar Marcus Aurelius Commodus Antoninus Augustus Armeniacus Medicus Parthicus Sarmaticus Germanicus Maximus, Hathur 7. Presented by me, Leonidas.

With which, perhaps, we may leave the Acts. There are, of course, multitudes of other intriguing archaeological details which interest the student of the book — scraps of the Via Egnatia, on which Paul trod, still visible at Philippi, the vast ruins of Ephesus, the stone pounder in the Liverpool Museum, which Charles Seltman[4] quite plausibly suggests may actually be the image of Artemis "fallen from heaven"

---

[4] *Riot in Ephesus,* pp. 86, 87.

of the Ephesian town clerk's speech. There is the stone dug from the wall in the Via Dolorosa, which is undoubtedly the notice threatening death to Gentiles who intruded in the sacred inner court of the Jerusalem Temple. There are altars "to the unknown gods," illustrative of Paul's Areopagus address, and the agora itself of Athens, laboriously excavated by the Americans since the Second World War, where Paul "disputed" with anyone who would listen to him. There is much which could be said of Tarsus, Antioch and Iconium, and much more will be discovered. Papyri, no doubt, will come to light further illustrating legal procedure. The story is only half told, and each new discovery runs true to form. It authenticates the New Testament, and shows the short-

THE CITY OF ATHENS, *showing the Stoa of Attalos (rebuilt) as viewed to the east across the agora.*

THE STOA OF ATTALOS *is an impressive sight when seen from inside the corridor.*

sightedness of the suspicion which has failed to see in the book a unique document of first century history.

Christ and Caesar

It is pleasant to meet the strong and refreshing challenge in the Sarum Lectures of 1960, 1961, of A. N. Sherwin-White. This Roman historian, writing with all the care, indeed with that distrust of unsupported evidence which is proper to his profession, is yet prompted to chide the unbalanced scepticism and fanciful theorizing of the New Testament "form critics." His restrained amazement at their conclusion that "the historical Christ is unknowable and the history of his mission cannot be written," while Roman historians pursue with convincing confidence the truth about the mission and person of Christ's "best-known contemporary," Tiberius Caesar, is a sobering comment on New Testament criticism, which is sane and long overdue. This is written of the gospels, while, says the same eminent authority, "for Acts the confirmation of historicity is overwhelming." It is archaeology which more than any other branch of learning and research, has made the remark possible.

ARCHAEOLOGY AND THE EPISTLES

CHAPTER 8

ARCHAEOLOGY
AND THE EPISTLES

Consideration of the light thrown on the epistolary literature of the New Testament by archaeological discovery brings us again to the Egyptian papyri. The fact that people in the ancient world wrote letters was, of course, well enough known from Latin literature before the Egyptian documents came to light. The letters of Cicero provide invaluable information on that stormy generation which saw the end of senatorial rule and the establishment of that dictatorship which we call the Roman Empire. The letters of Pliny show Roman society at its best at the turn of the first century of the Christian era. Its surviving books contain Pliny's official communications with the Emperor Trajan when the writer was governor of Bithynia, and much information, as we have seen, about the first clash between the State and the Church.

Literacy in the First Century

The letters of both Romans survive in their own right as literature. The surprise of the papyri has been the vast extent of ancient literacy, and the volume of the everyday correspondence between private persons on all manner of subjects of daily interest. The letters of the New Testament, although at times they touch the heights of literary power, have as their prime object information and exhortation in the plain and simple speech which "the common people hear gladly." And the discovery of Egypt's mass of proletarian correspondence, besides providing much linguistic information, has shown the class of writing to which the letters of Paul, Peter, John, Jude and James belong.

Consider for example the breadth of the subject matter. The papyrus letters cover the whole range of life. Many are not without humor and intense humanity. There is, for example, little Theon. Who was Theon? A mere boy, who has the honor of a catalog reference in a collection of select papyri: *"Theon (spoilt boy), letter of, p. 297."*

Theon, at any rate, wrote a letter to his father, sixteen hundred years ago, and from it one may judge:

Theon to Theon his father greeting. You did a fine thing not taking me with you to town. If you won't take me with you to Alexandria, I won't write you a letter, or speak to you, or wish you good-day. And if you go to Alexandria I won't hold your hand, nor speak to you ever again. If you won't take me that's what's up! Mother said to Archelaus, "He upsets me, take him away!" It was nice of you to send me presents, big ones, beans, on the 12th, the day you sailed. Send me a lyre, please do. If you don't, I won't eat, and I won't drink. There now! I pray for your health.

And after that he signs himself by his pet name, Theonas. "Your little Tommy," so to speak! Did Theon starve to death, or did his father send for him? Probably, we can safely picture "Theonas" in the boulevards of Alexandria, free from inhibitions and developing his little ego.

Several schoolboys appear in the papyri of the same century. There is one from a neglected little lad named Thonis. The exquisitely human touch in the closing words seems to bring him very close to us:

To my lord and father Arion, from Thonis, greeting. I pray for you every day. Look, this is my fifth letter to you, and you have written to me only once, nor have you come to see me. You promised me saying, "I am coming," but you have not come to find out whether my teacher is looking after me or not. And he himself asks every day saying, "Isn't he coming yet?" And I just say, "Yes." Try then to come quickly, that he may teach me as he really wants to do. And when you come, remember what I have often written to you about. Good-bye my lord and father, and may you prosper many years along with my brothers, whom may the evil eye harm not. Remember my pigeons. To Arion from Thonis.

In another family it was the father not the son, who worried about the fees. It is easy to imagine what sort of a letter from home young Aurelius was answering, when he addressed his "very sweetest father." "I pray for you," he continues, "every day to the local deities. Do not be worried, father, about my studies. I am working hard and taking relaxation. It will be all right with me. I greet my

THE SEALED LETTERS *(left) consist of sheets of papyrus rolled, tied, and sealed, ready for delivery. The typical private letter (right) was written in large semi-cursive handwriting.*

mother. . . ." The letter then proceeds for a dozen lines with enthusiastic greetings to friends and relatives, a safer subject. Aurelius senior would doubtless have preferred some assurance about the relaxation.

There were other parents prepared to cut their worries at the root. There is a famous papyrus letter dated actually from 1 B.C. which is a comment on the grim, hard world to which Christ came with a charter for children. Hilarion, in search of work in Alexandria, writes to his wife Alis at Oxyrhynchus. He addresses her as "sister," a term of endearment, though cognate marriage between brother and sister was permissible in Egypt. The text runs:

> Hilarion to his sister Alis very many greetings, likewise to my lady Berous and Apollonarion. Know that we are still in Alexandria. Do not be anxious; if they really go home, I will remain in Alexandria. I beg and entreat you, take care of the little one, and as soon as we receive our pay I will send it up to you. If by chance you bear a child, if it is a boy, let it be, if it is a girl, cast it out. You have said to Aphrodisias "Do not forget me." How can I forget you? I beg you then not to be anxious. The 29th year of Caesar, Pauni 23. (Addressed): Deliver to Alis from Hilarion.

There is something peculiarly horrible about the casual directions for the exposure and murder of a babe in the context of an affectionate letter.

Subject Range and Format

From schoolboys we might move to soldiers on campaign, husbands away from home, officials on circuit, absent friends, and the host who, in any year, use pen and paper to record their thoughts. To pigeons, presents and school fees, we might have added the problems and concerns of anxious wives, busy builders, solicitous hosts and grateful guests. And does not Paul himself range in subject from delicate irony over Corinthian pretensions to stern rebuke for heresy, and from news of friends to the warm cloak he left at Troas, and some precious books?

There is no perceptible difference between the style of the private letters of the first and the fourth century. They are innumerable, and repay the careful examination of the New Testament scholar. It is revealed, for example, that Paul observed with some care the forms of polite address common in his day. There is an opening word of salutation, followed by thanksgiving and prayer for the person or company addressed. Then comes the special subject of communication, greetings to friends, and perhaps a closing word of prayer.

Even Thonis' letter to Arion reveals some of these stereotyped forms, and they are almost universal. Here is a second-century letter which shows strikingly the Pauline style in brief:

> Ammonous to her sweetest father, greeting. When I received your letter and recognized that by the will of the gods you were preserved, I rejoiced greatly. And as at the same time an opportunity here presented itself, I am writing you this letter being anxious to pay my respects. Attend as quickly as possible to the matters that are pressing. Whatever the little one asks shall be done. If the bearer of this letter hands over a small basket to you, it is I who sent it. All your friends greet you by name. Celer greets you and all who are with him. I pray for your health.

The Professional Letter-writer

One other point of some importance emerges from a study of the papyrus letters, and that is the presence and function of the scribe. Letters were dictated, and even men and women quite capable of adding a signature and postscript in their own hand appear to have employed a professional letter-writer for the body of their note. In the epistle to the Galatians, Paul, in closing, took the pen from the scribe, and "in large characters" (6:11) paid the church which he had so sternly reprimanded the compliment of a personal postscript above the signature which authenticated the whole.

It has been suggested that a capable scribe, aware of the mind of the writer of the letter, may have been entrusted, like any capable secretary today, with supplying some supplementary information. Slight differences of style (as for example between the first and second letters of Peter) might easily be accounted for by the scribe's own phraseology in filling out a sketchy direction. One important lesson, therefore, of the letters from the papyri, is the limitations of stylistic criticism, especially of the modern computer-ridden variety.

The Language of the New Testament Clarified

In the sphere of language the papyri have given much light to the student of the New Testament epistles, and to the book as a whole. The non-literary papyri have revealed that Paul and his fellow-writers used the vernacular of the day and the racy speech of common communication. What else could be expected? The politician, the demagogue and agitator have always realized the need to speak to people in the terms and patterns of their familiar intercourse. The aim of the New Testament writers is to be taken seriously, and its writers in consequence deliberately use the speech of ordinary folk in their daily round. Luke begins his gospel with a piece of elaborate Greek worthy of Thucydides. Then as though in demonstrable and deliberate renunciation of all literary artifice, he rounds off his sentence and adopts the vernacular.

The same vernacular, recovered from the papyri, is the speech of the New Testament letters, and indeed of the gospels. It is not without grace and power; it is not incapable of poetry, as more than one chapter of Paul demonstrates. At the same time, it is in the full stream of contemporary Greek. And it is the vocabulary of that contemporary language which has thrown light on passages in the epistles obscure to the scholars who, before the coming of papyrology, approached the text only from the angle of classical and literary Greek.

Here are some illustrations from the sizeable list of new words and new meanings which the papyri have added to the Greek lexicon. "I have all, and abound," runs Philippians 4:18 in KJV. But why a compound form of the verb "to have," which, in Classical Greek, carries a meaning which would not make sense in the passage quoted, any more than it would in Matthew 6:2, 5, and 16? "Verily," Christ says, in both places, "they have their reward." In translating the Aramaic, Matthew used the same compound of the verb "to have" as that which appears in the Pauline passage. Matthew's meaning was plain enough from the other gospels, but why such a strange word? There was no answer until hosts of bills were found in the rubbish heaps of an Egyptian town — only some of them paid. The formula for receipt was the verb in question — "he is quit." Matthew was again in imagination at the receipt of customs when he penned his verse. Whimsically he pictured the hypocrite's bill, his claim on God paid in full in earthly glory, spot cash. "He is quit," he wrote. And Paul is saying: "I give you a receipt in full for all your kindness." How much more vivid the passage becomes by the recovered metaphor.

So, too, does Hebrews 11:1 when a papyrus document reveals that the word so vaguely translated "substance," was a word for "title-deeds." Title-deeds give secure possession of that which is not necessarily seen, and thus faith firmly places in our hands the unseen wealth of a spiritual world. For the same world Paul counted all worldly advantage "loss" (Philippians 3:8). His expression gains strength when a papyrus uses the same word for bones cast out for the dogs.

When the Jews of Thessalonica complain that "those who have turned the world upside down" have arrived to disturb their peace (Acts 17:6), they use a word Paul himself employs of those who are "unsettling" the folk of Galatia (Galatians 5:12). This is the very word which Theon the schoolboy quotes in the letter mentioned earlier in this chapter: "He upsets me," the distracted mother complained.

In Romans 8:23, the word *aparche* is translated in KJV, in accordance with its classical meaning "first fruits." It was a word for the first seasonal offerings to the gods. In a papyrus document, however, it has the meaning of "legacy duty," and in another it signifies the fee demanded for citizenship. In yet another context it clearly means "birth certificate," and this would provide a convincing and illuminating rendering for Romans 8:23. The Christian has a birth certificate of the Spirit. The metaphor is not remote from that suggested for Hebrews 11:1.

The new light from the papyri suggests, in consequence, numerous more exact translations. For example, read "originator," for "captain" in Hebrews 2:10, "debating" for "doubting" in I Timothy 2:8, and "I have guarded my trust" for "I have kept the faith" in II Timothy 4:7. Examples might be multiplied, but enough has been quoted to show that, with the discovery of the papyri, the language of the New Testament has truly risen from the dead.

ARCHAEOLOGY AND THE
APOCALYPSE

CHAPTER 9

ARCHAEOLOGY
AND THE APOCALYPSE

RUIN-MUSING, AS OLD AS ISAIAH AND AS MODERN AS H. V. Morton and the holiday cruise of affluent societies, finds rich food for its fancy near the Turkish village of Seljuk. Nearby stand the stones of Ephesus, the scene of nearly eighty years of digging. Rose Macaulay,[1] who has made a fascinating collection of the ruin-literature of travelers and poets, quotes Richard Chandler who visited Asia Minor two and a half centuries ago. "Returning from this cavity," wrote this eager clergyman concerning the swamp, where he thought he had found the temple of Artemis, the "Diana" of the vivid story of Acts 19, "the traveler has nothing else in view but venerable heaps of rubbish, and must be forced to supply his curiosity with considering that this was the place where once stood and flourished that renowned wonder of the world."

One of H. V. Morton's most colorful chapters[2] tells how at Seljuk he found a stagnant pond, lush with waterweed, from which protruded sculptured capitals and carved column

---

[1] *The Pleasure of Ruins*, p. 235.
[2] *In the Steps of Saint Paul*, pp. 320-340.

drums. Here he imagined the summer frogs croaking in derision: "Great is Diana, great is Diana," for the mud-buried marble is all that is left of the great temple of the mystery cult which kept ten thousand priestess courtesans employed.

Ephesus

Ephesus lay at the mouth of the Cayster between the Koressos Range and the sea. Like all the river valleys around the great blunt end of the Asian continent's westward protrusion, that of the Cayster was the terminal of a trade route which linked with other roads converging and branching out towards the separated civilizations and tribes of the East and the Asian steppes. This was why Ephesus was chosen by the early Ionian colonists from Athens as a site for their colony. The Greeks called a colony an "emporion," or a "way in," because their concept of such settlement was that of a gateway by which an active self-governing community

MARBLE STREET OF EPHESUS *as viewed to the west from the agora.*

could tap the trade of a foreign hinterland. Ephesus filled the role precisely.

By New Testament times, however, the great days of Ephesus' trade were past. Like her rival Miletus, similarly located at the end of the Maeander valley, thirty miles to the south, Ephesus had difficulty with her harbor, the essential gateway to the sea. Deforestation has been mankind's ancient folly, and no part of the Mediterranean world has suffered worse than Asia Minor. The quest for timber and charcoal, overgrazing, and the destructiveness of the Mediterranean goat, eternally nibbling and trampling the regenerating forest, denuded the hinterland. Topsoil slipped from the bared hillsides, streams became swamps, and the stormwaters reached the sea laden with silt, which choked the harbors. The harbor-works of Ephesus may be traced today seven miles from the sea. Where once a sheltered waterway formed a safe haven, there is now a reedy plain. Sir William Ramsay, most factual of archaeologists, speaks in awe of the "uncanny volume of sound" which, in his day at the turn of the century, greeted the evening visitor to the desolate levels where Ephesus once harbored her ships.

She was, nonetheless, over many centuries, fortunate in her engineers. The winding Maeander was silting up the harbor of Miletus as early as 500 B.C., and when that city suffered irreparable damage in the Persian suppression of the great revolt of the Ionian Greek cities, the choking up of her waterway passed beyond repair. It was Ephesus' opportunity, and a succession of rulers promoted the maintenance of the harbor facilities which the increased volume of trade and traffic demanded.

The kings of Pergamum, most dynamic and powerful of the lesser successor-states of Alexander's divided empire, did much for Ephesus, and when the Romans inherited the kingdom of Pergamum by the will of its last ruler, Attalus III, they continued the policy of promoting Ephesian trade. The Romans took up the legacy of Pergamum in 133 B.C. and used

Ephesus as the proconsul's seat. The city was proud of its name, "the Landing Place," and the title is found on a coin as late as the third century of the Christian era. It is, perhaps, significant that the same coin bears the image of a small oar-propelled boat, an official's "barge," not the deep-hulled merchant-men which mark the city's pride in her sea-borne trade on the coins of earlier centuries. Paul's ship made no call there in A.D. 57.

Domitian, at the end of the first century, appears to have been the last ruler to attempt to repair the harbor of Ephesus, but trade had obviously declined two centuries before. By the time of Justinian, five centuries later, the battle with sand, silt and mud was lost, and Ephesus was falling to ruins in a swampy terrain. Justinian, to be sure, built a church to Saint John on the site, in part compensation perhaps for the looting of the green stone columns from Artemis' temple for the vast church of Saint Sophia in Byzantium, or Constantinople as the city was then called. They may still be seen by visitors to the great basilica in Istanbul.

Deepening economic depression and decline were therefore the background of Ephesus' life over the period of the New Testament. If the spirit of a community seeps into a church and determines, in some fashion, its outlook and its testimony, Ephesus provides an illustration, for the stone foundations of jetty and dockside warehouse, deep inland on the edge of the desolate plain, are sharp light on the city whose Christians were bidden be mindful whence they had fallen, and do as they once did, where old things had passed away and ahead lay death.

The Church in Ephesus

The last glimpse of Ephesus shown in the New Testament reveals an aging church, in need of an infusion of new life. Hence the closing detail of imagery in the apocalyptic letter. Coins of Ephesus sometimes show a date palm, sacred to Artemis, and the symbol of the goddess' beneficent activity. "I will give him," writes John, "to eat of the tree of life." It was not to be. Ignatius, writing a generation later, still accords the church high praise. It became a seat of bishops, and a notable council was held there as late as A.D. 431. Then came long decline. The coast, with continual soil erosion of the hinterland, became malarial. The Turks came with ruin for Asia. The church died with the city. The "candlestick" was removed out of its place.

Archaeology, nonetheless, has shown that the prestige, and indeed the magnificence of the city, long outlived its declining usefulness as a seaport. Under Claudius, in the middle of the first century, and under Trajan at the beginning of the second, the great theater was remodeled. It was under Claudius that the monumental Marble Street was built. Nero gave Ephesus a stadium. Domitian widened and beautified the great central boulevard. Adornment continued till the days of the Gothic raid in A.D. 263. It is obvious that Paul's vision had picked on one of the strategic centers of the world.

THE HUGE THEATER OF EPHESUS, *carved from this hillside (center of photo), seated 25,000 people.*

Smyrna

Youthful Smyrna was Ephesus' rival, and to Smyrna's enduring church was promised a "crown of life." The Christian would fasten on the words with satisfaction, for it was the sort of poet's tag on which cities preen themselves. Athens was "violet-crowned," until men tired of the adjective. Of Auckland, New Zealand, where these words are written, to its citizens' delight, Kipling wrote, "last, loneliest, loveliest, exquisite, apart." In such fashion the simile of a crown dominates all praise of Smyrna.

AT SMYRNA, *these columns mark the past splendor of the forum.*

"The city has been styled," writes the Rev. Chandler in his eighteenth-century account, "the crown of Ionia." More significantly Aristides calls the "Golden Street," which ringed Mount Pagus with lovely buildings, "the crown of Ariadne in the heavenly constellation." Apollonius of Tyana, amid rich praise for Smyrna, says rhetorically that it is greater charm "to wear a crown of men than a crown of porticoes."

From afar, the crest of Mount Pagus, its broken ruins

cleared by the diligent spades of modern digging, still faintly
suggests a diadem above the city's crest. "I have been up
there," wrote Freya Stark, "sometimes to walk in the morning, with Ionia on one side and Aeolis on the other, spread
below; and nearby, in a shapeless depression, the stadium
where Polycarp was burned, and have thought of that old
bishop how he would describe his intercourse with John,
and with the rest of those who had seen the Lord. . . ." Under
"the crown of Smyrna," Polycarp was not the only Christian
who won "a crown of life."

Pergamum

Pergamum, royally situated in a commanding position,
with a view of far ranges, the sea, and the purple peaks of
Lesbos, had been, when John wrote, a city-seat of government for full four hundred years. It was a capital city in
pre-Roman days, and when the last of her kings, as was
mentioned above, bequeathed his kingdom to the Romans in
133 B.C., Pergamum became the chief town of the new province of Asia. It was natural then that the first temple of the
imperial cult, the worship of the emperor on which the Christians looked with such deep abhorrence, should be located
here. A temple to Rome and Augustus was erected in
Pergamum in 29 B.C. So "the worship of the Beast," as the
uncompromising imagery of Revelation describes it, came to
Asia. But other cults beside that of Rome were endemic at
Pergamum. There was the worship of Asklepios, the god
of healing, whose symbol was a serpent. A coin of Pergamum
shows the Emperor Caracalla standing spear in hand before
a great serpent coiled around a bending sapling. The emperor raises his right hand in the exact gesture of the Nazi
salute, which is, in fact, one of the most ancient of all
gestures of adoration. A prayer as old as Psalm 144 calls for
rescue "from these alien hordes with lies upon their lips
and the right hand raised in a false oath."

The letter to Pergamum is addressed to "those who dwell

AT PERGAMUM *are the remains of the throne-like altar to Zeus, which invited the description "Satan's Seat" by early Christians because of its dominant position above the city.*

where Satan's seat is," and Christians must have found something peculiarly satanic in the town's preoccupation with the serpent image. Pausanias the Greek traveler, who wrote many descriptions of ancient cities, spoke of Asklepios as "sitting on a throne with a staff in his hand, and his other hand upon the head of a serpent." The church in Pergamum must have found the surrounding symbolism of paganism quite diabolical.

"Satan's Seat"

Pausanias also mentions the magnificent throne-like altar to Zeus, which stood on the crag dominating the city, and which is now in East Berlin. The altar commemorated the defeat of a Gallic invasion of Asia. Recovered by German archaeologists, the great block of decorated stone was taken to Berlin where it forms a major exhibit in the East Berlin Museum, rebuilt after the fashion of twenty centuries ago in a huge silent hall, cunningly lighted. Its base is more than forty yards long and nearly forty wide; it rises to a height of perhaps fifty feet. In form it might be the entrance to some gigantic temple. Above three sides of the base a graceful colonnade runs, set with dozens of slender pillars. A flight of twenty-six wide marble steps rises up to its center, which contains a small sanctuary. Immediately below the colonnade are set the friezes which are the altar's chief glory.

They tell the story of the legendary struggle between the gods and goddesses of Olympus and the giants. Athene, her face long since obliterated, clutches the hair of a rising giant. Hekate thrusts a torch into the face of another, and there stands Artemis, her shattered arm still poised to hold a bow. The giants, in accordance with Pergamum's prevailing obsession, are represented as a brood of Titans, with snake-like tails. Curiously enough, examination by experts from the British Museum of the battered marble figure of a giant, which has been lying for some years in the junk yard of the Worksop Town Council in a London suburb, has led to a

PERGAMUM'S ALTAR TO ZEUS *has been reconstructed and is now displayed in the East Berlin Museum.*

startling conclusion. The statue may be one of the missing figures from the frieze surrounding the altar of Zeus.

This Zeus, to whom the throne-like altar was dedicated, was called Zeus the Saviour, and the title would impress Christian minds as peculiarly blasphemous. They must have called the altar "Satan's seat," and so put the phrase in the Apocalypse. "No wonder," writes Moffat, "Pergamum was called the throne of Satan by early Christians who revolted against the splendid and insidious paganism of the place. . . . Least of all in this cathedral center of the imperial cult could dissent be tolerated."

But how did the giant from "Satan's seat" get to London's Worksop? Some careful sleuthing appears to establish the fact it came from Asia over two centuries ago to form part of the collection of the Earl of Arundel, and fell on evil days when Worksop Manor, the Arundel seat, was broken up.

Thyatira

Inscriptions are grist for the archaeologist's mill, and from Thyatira, fourth of the cities of the Apocalypse, they come in plenty. Thyatira's valley was a broad and ancient highway of trade, and in the days of the Roman Peace the city became, like Laodicea, a center of busy commerce. More trade guilds, those ubiquitous associations of businessmen and craftsmen, have been identified in Thyatira than in any other Asian city. Inscriptions mention workers in wool, linen, leather, and bronze, dyers, tanners, potters and bakers.

The people of Thyatira's church were thus drawn from a commercial community, alive to salesmanship, keen to do business, and alert to capture trade. Lydia, it will be remembered, when she met Paul in distant Macedonia, was a Thyatiran abroad with purple cloth to sell. The trade guilds must have been an anxious problem to the Christian craftsman. How could he attend the formal meetings and banquets without witnessing licentiousness and condoning pagan rites? It was the old Corinthian problem of "sitting at meat in the idol's temple" which confronted the struggling church. Archaeology, with its revelation of the scope of the city's trade organization, has set the moral dilemma in high relief. But as with Philadelphia and Laodicea, little more than preliminary surveys have been carried out for the excavation of Thyatira. Systematic archaeological investigation has obviously much more to say on John's seven churches.

Sardis

Sardis, however, has received some attention from the archaeologists. As early as 1910, the American, H. C. Butler, with a magnificently equipped expedition, worked on the site. The great crane which was used for lifting large blocks of stone lay rusting in the ruins for many years, as its own contribution to the wilderness, after the "dig" was abandoned in 1914. Harvard and Cornell universities are at present continuing the good work. Sardis' temple of Artemis has been uncovered. It appears that under the influence of the

AT THE SITE OF ANCIENT SARDIS, *standing pillars dominate the ruins of the Temple of Artemis.*

Cybele-cult of Ephesus, that goddess was associated with Artemis in joint worship. It was an unfinished building and has no significance in the interpretation of John's apocalyptic letter, save that a cross cut here and there into the stone shows that the pagan shrine was converted to Christian purposes. The remains of a brick chapel are also visible in the ruin. A mortgage deed, dated some three centuries before Christ, gives some idea of the wealth of the temple. One Mnesimachus acknowledges a huge gold loan, and specifies whole villages in security.

Apocalyptic Imagery and Archaeology

Relevant to the archaeology of the Apocalypse are the ruins of the Roman Tiber port of Ostia. In the "taunt-song" of Chapter 18, John pictures destruction falling on the Babylon of the Seven Hills, and the lament of the Mediterranean traders who no longer, in that day of judgment, will discharge their cargoes there. It was at Ostia that the ships unloaded, and the great warehouses still stand, their gaunt ruins two and three stories high. There are the remains, too, of tenement blocks and a Christian church.

In concluding this chapter there remains a brief word to say on Chapter 13, most horrific of the visions of the Apocalypse. Two points find some illustration from archaeology, the seal of the Beast, and the number of his name.

In the papyri, "to be sealed" meant to be imperially protected and retained for imperial use. This appears to be the use of the verb which Paul had in mind in Romans 15:28, a verse which has produced an astonishing variety of renderings. Paul seems to mean: "When I have secured this fruit for them to hold and to retain." Seals were set, in pursuance of this practice, on sacks of grain to guarantee the correct weight or measure of the contents. There was also a mark, a red stamp, which was required for all documents of exchange. It showed the Emperor's name and the year of his reign, and was technically known as "the seal."

If, therefore, the first and basic interpretation of the Beast is Caesar himself, John's picture of the seal stamping hand and brow of the duped multitude becomes shockingly true to life. They are stamped and sealed with the sign of the false god of Rome, stamped upon the hand which creates, and before the brain which plans. And without the stamp, which stands symbolically for conformity, and tacit acceptance of the worship and divinity of the Emperor, a man could "neither buy nor sell." The trade guilds with their stranglehold upon a man's livelihood, and the success of his daily avocation, are, of course, in view. This somber century, in which the battle for liberty has been fought over again in three continents, and still continues to be fought in large tracts of the globe, has produced many illustrations of the tyranny over hand and head, and the despot's threat to livelihood and thought, which John thus symbolized.

And what of the last verse in the chapter: ". . . his number is six hundred and sixty-six"? Note first that a far from negligible manuscript tradition gives 616, not 666. In both Greek and Latin the letters of the alphabet had numerical value, and the fact was very commonly used to build puzzles. Among the wall scratchings from Pompeii is an election notice in which the vowels are cryptically exchanged for numbers, and another inscription speaks of a girl called Harmonia. "The number of her name," it says, "is 45." The key to the puzzle seems to be that Harmonia suggests the nine Muses, and 45 is the sum of all the digits from 1 to 9.

The churches of Asia probably knew the key to 666 or 616, but it was early forgotten. In Greek 616 adds up to "Caesar God," but 666 is not so simple, and much ingenuity and juggling with spelling has been employed to fit the number to "Nero Caesar," or "Caius Caesar." It is also plausibly suggested that 666 falls short of the perfect trinity 777 in all counts, and thus presents a grisly picture of the power and baseness of Antichrist. Archaeology has thus done no more than point the way. The subject remains open for conjecture and ingenuity. After all the writer warns his readers: "Behold here is wisdom." Perhaps some papyrus scrap, still undiscovered or undeciphered, some inscription under a Turkish doorstep or embedded in a wall, contains an answer to John's cryptogram.

The key to the interpretation of the Apocalypse is, of course, the significance of its imagery. Much of that imagery is Old Testament in its origin; much of it, as the illustrations in this chapter have briefly shown, is based on contemporary history and geography. Some of it, it may be fairly admitted, is still elusive, and it is here that archaeology may still have something of interest and importance to say.

Archaeology is no longer a Western preserve. There are indigenous schools of archaeologists in Bible lands, which are doing, and will no doubt continue to do good work. Asia Minor, scene of the earliest activities of the organized Church, still offers vast scope for investigation and discovery. The Apocalypse is a document of early Church history, and as such will yet yield more of its primary meaning, as spade and trowel bring to clearer light the ways of thought and action in the first century.[3]

---

[3] The cities of Revelation are dealt with at greater length in *The Cities of the New Testament* by E. M. Blaiklock (Pickering and Inglis).

THE NEW TESTAMENT AND
THE DEAD SEA SCROLLS

CHAPTER 10

THE NEW TESTAMENT AND THE DEAD SEA SCROLLS

THE FAMOUS DEAD SEA SCROLLS ARE AS RELEVANT TO THE study of the New Testament as they are to the understanding of the Old, and any account of New Testament archaeology would be incomplete without some mention of their significance. It is more than a score of years since the library of the Qumran sect was discovered in the caves by the bitter Dead Sea, and since 1947 the story has been told often. It is more than the tale of the shepherd boy, the flung stone, and the rattle of shattered pottery which heralded the amazing find. It is also a story of scholarly tenacity, sheer courage, meticulous research and devotion on the part of Western scholars, as John C. Trever's enthralling book of 1966 demonstrated so well.[1]

Current Discovery

Nor is the story complete. Late in 1967 Israeli archaeologist and soldier, Yigael Yadin, announced the discovery of a new scroll, the longest yet to come to light. It was in the

[1] *The Untold Story of Qumran* (Pickering and Inglis).

135

QUMRAN CAVE 4 *as seen from a distance, and closeup.*
Archaeologists found scrolls on the floor of the cave.

possession of a Bethlehem antique dealer, and fell into Israeli hands after the Six Days' War. Less than one-tenth of a millimeter thick, the parchment is in extremely fragile condition; insects had begun to gnaw at its fringes, and the outer portion, said Yadin, looked like "melted chocolate." Unrolled, the scroll measures over twenty-eight feet in length, more than four feet longer than Qumran's complete scroll of Isaiah.

The scroll is dated from 50 B.C. to the beginning of the 1st century A.D., but it could be a copy of a work written earlier during the Second Temple period: "From the external evidence," Yadin says, "it is apparent that the author definitely wanted his scroll to be taken as the law of God." Unlike all other apocryphal writings of the time, the new scroll is written as though God Himself is speaking, and giving detailed instructions for the maintenance of the Temple. It was the same Yigael Yadin who discovered three years earlier the Genesis scroll in the ruins of the great fortress of Masada. None of these finds have any New Testament significance. They merely whet the appetite for what may yet come to light.

Fragmented or amazingly intact, all these ancient documents may be seen in the Archaeological Museum of the Old City of Jerusalem, or in Israel's Shrine of the Scrolls. They are carefully preserved under regulated conditions of temperature and humidity, for the nations have learned that it is a mark of civilization to cherish all links with the past.

The Scrolls and the Critics

Few documents have been so intensively studied, and few so recklessly interpreted. Christian and non-Christian have had their say. Modern systems of thought with some interest in eliminating the influence of Christianity and the abiding challenge of its Founder, have asserted that the teaching of the little sect which hid its books in the caves disposes of both. It is ten or eleven years, for example, since

Komsomolskaya Pravda, the organ of the Soviet Communist Youth movement, alleged that the scrolls proved that Jesus never existed. It is strange to find John Allegro, in syndicated newspaper articles, repeating the assertion, and seeing in the Scrolls "a challenge to the Church far greater than was ever presented by Darwin's theory of evolution. . . ." The comparison is apt, and a trifle naive. Stripped of bilateral hysteria, Darwin's theory never was a challenge to the Church. Neither are the Scrolls, deeply disappointing though that may be to the minority of critics who, from the first century until today, have been eager to show that Christianity was a lamentable mistake.

The strange myth that Christians are afraid of some disconcerting revelation in the documents, dies hard. In a footnote to his terse and authoritative summary of the most recent and mature conclusions of the subject of the Scrolls,[2] Professor F. F. Bruce talks of a meeting of the Society for New Testament Studies in 1955. Bruce read a paper on the Scrolls. It was not the only contribution on the theme, and discussion was wide and animated. It was therefore with some interest, writes Bruce ironically, that he read some weeks later Edmund Wilson's popular account in which he remarks: "New Testament scholars have almost without exception boycotted the whole subject of the Scrolls." Nothing could be further from the truth. It is odd to find the legend in the headlines eleven years later still.

The texts from the caves are varied provender. There were manuscripts of Old Testament books, a thousand years older than anything which scholarship had hitherto possessed. There were commentaries on the prophets, of no great value. There was a "manual of discipline," from which it is possible to gain some notion of the life lived in the desert community. There was a strange mystic story of a war between "the children of light" and the forces of darkness,

---

[2] *Second Thoughts on the Dead Sea Scrolls* (Paternoster Press), p. 138.

with some allusion to a "teacher of righteousness" done to death by the hierarchy.

The Teacher of Righteousness

This mysterious figure at first gave rise to some controversy. As far as substance can be given to the shadowy personality, the Teacher was probably the founder of the sect, a good man who rose in protest against the corruption of religion, and met the martyrdom which such saints have too commonly encountered in man's somber story. To identify him with Christ, who died in the full blaze of recorded history, is only to demonstrate the eagerness of some to diminish at all costs the historicity of the Founder of the Christian faith. Nor did the people of Qumran think of their Teacher of Righteousness as a messiah. In their odd eschatology, in fact, while they regarded themselves, in some sense, as the corporate fulfillment of Isaiah's "Servant" and Daniel's "Son of Man," they looked for the appearance, at the end of the age, of three figures, a priestly messiah, a military messiah, and Moses' "prophet." Such speculation is of small significance. But critics hostile to Christianity, in the first extravagances of interpretation, thought they had discovered the real origins of Christianity. It passes understanding how anyone could imagine that the blurred and elusive Teacher could be the reality, and the tremendous figure of Christ, whose record has daunted mankind, could be a legend based on him.

Some ingenuity has been more legitimately expended in attempts to identify the Teacher and his chief persecutor, the "Wicked Priest," with known historical figures. It cannot be claimed that any conclusive identification has been reached, but it is ludicrous to see the crime of the collaborating priesthood, so starkly described in the gospels, as being in any way a rendering of the fate of the Teacher of Righteousness. More than one noble person has been done to death by vested interests, religious and political.

The Qumran Community and Christ

It is also true that some of the sectarian expressions may be found in the utterances of Christ, but surely a teacher of the common people of the land, whom they "heard gladly," would be expected to seek a vocabulary close to that of contemporary religious usage. The fact that the imagery of light and darkness, so common in John's writings, phrases like "eternal life," and the double "amen," or "verily, verily I say . . ." appear in the Scrolls, only demonstrates that Christ spoke the common language of His day. It was Christ's way to emphasize old truth and set it in a more compelling light. In precisely the same way Paul adapted and appropriated the terminology of the "mystery religions."

It is also worth noting that, in direct contrast with the rigid discipline of the sectaries, Christ was no ascetic. His foes held that against Him. He also contradicted their ethical teaching, notably in His firm command to love one's enemies. Qumran counseled hate for "the foe of light." "Love the

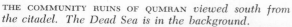

THE COMMUNITY RUINS OF QUMRAN *viewed south from the citadel. The Dead Sea is in the background.*

Children of Light," runs the Qumran text, "and hate the Children of Darkness." It is a behest from the allegorical document found among the Scrolls, "The War of the Children of Light and the Children of Darkness," a curious compilation built out of the detailed study of the Old Testament wars, and what appears to have been a Roman military manual. Nothing could be more alien to Christ's teaching. Indeed He was surely quoting when He said: "You have heard it said: Thou shalt love thy neighbour and hate thine enemy, but I say to you . . . ."

In short, it is historically impossible to identify the well-documented life of Christ with the exotic allegorizing of the desert sect. Kevin Smyth, the Jesuit scholar, remarks that to compare the scrolls with the New Testament is "like comparing a fish and a man because both are wet after coming out of the sea." And against those who see in Qumran the soil from which Christianity sprang, he says: "Rather it was from the soil such as this that sprang the thorns which tried to choke the seed of the Gospel." Kevin Smyth is perhaps overemphatic, for, traced up and through John the Baptist, dissident Essenism, of which Qumran was a facet, may, in fact, be granted a place in pre-Christian history. Its measure of good was taken, absorbed and interpreted in Christian attitudes and thought. But Christ was the majestic center of the new faith.

The Gospels — Superior Documents of the Ancient World

Those who are emotionally committed to the anti-Christian view are in difficulties with the gospels. To say, as Allegro does, that "there is no worthwhile contemporary evidence outside the New Testament that Jesus ever existed," is no contribution to discussion. The four words "outside the New Testament" strip the assertion of meaning. Historians would be glad to have evidence so authentic, so multiple, so congruent, on more than one personality and event of ancient history.

The evidence of the Anglo-Saxon irruption into Britain is confined to a few score words in the Venerable Bede. The evidence of Julius Caesar's reconnaissance across the Channel in 55 B.C., a date which every schoolboy used to know, is principally in Caesar's own words, in a document designed to justify his military career. The existence of the English, like the existence of the Church, has a certain verificatory force. . . .

The gospels, however scholars may disagree on this detail or that, are obviously documents of ancient history. A papyrus fragment from the last of them to be written is to be seen in a Manchester University library. It is palaeographically dated in the first generation of the second century. The first account of the life of Christ is reliably dated in the middle sixties of the first century. Myths do not grow thus in historically documented ages, and such methods of interpretation vanished from responsible scholarship in the nineteenth century. The classical historian is perpetually amazed at the methods of interpretation tolerated in New Testament scholarship, which would be dismissed as absurd in any other branch of historical study. A letter in the *Times* of London, in 1965, on the subject of the Scrolls, a statement signed by six Old Testament scholars of professional rank, shows that such amazement is not confined to classicists.

When the little band at Qumran fled before the cohorts who were mopping up the pockets of resistance in the lower Jordan valley, Christianity was already established in the major centers from Alexandria to Antioch and Rome. It was perhaps in A.D. 68 that the patrols found and burnt Qumran. That was the last year of Nero's principate. Four years earlier, Nero had made the Christians of Rome — "a vast number," according to Tacitus, the historian — the scapegoats for Rome's great fire. Almost twenty years earlier, if the Nazareth Decree is rightly judged a rescript of Claudius, Nero's imperial predecessor had heard the Pharisees' explanation of the empty tomb. Seven years earlier still, the same Claudius, as we have seen, had chided the Jews of

NEAR THE QUMRAN RUINS *is this view to the south, looking down the wadi to Ain Feshka in the distance. At right is the marl cliff containing Cave 4.*

Alexandria for turbulence, and appears to make a reference to Christian missionaries. But these are trifles. The career of Paul of Tarsus, heir of three cultures, ranked for intellect by T. R. Glover, the great classical scholar, with Plato himself,[3] had ended before Qumran went its pathetic way.

It soon became apparent, as scholars went to work on Qumran and its library, that the true interest and meaning of the discovery lay in the ruin, as much as in the caves, in the people, as much as in the Scrolls. But the study of the community of Qumran really added little to that which was plain for all to see in the New Testament. It merely sharpened vision and understanding. Two other discoveries may serve as illustrations: All visitors to Stonehenge today can see a typical short-bladed Mycenaean dagger carved on one of the upright stones. It was picked up by photography in 1952, but had been there 3500 years. No one saw it until it was pointed out. Now it is obvious to all. It was known

[3] *Paul of Tarsus*, 1925, p. 1.

in many a biological laboratory that mildew killed the bacteria on the plates, long before penicillin was invented.

It is thus with the Scrolls. Most of what they reveal was plain in the gospels, but few had seen the historical truth until the study of the Qumran society enlivened understanding.

The "Third Force" in Palestine

The Pharisees and Sadducees dominate the gospel story. The first named were the defenders and exponents of the Law, the second a cynical priestly hierarchy, collaborators and simonists. Both hated Christ, the former because He exposed the hypocrisy of their legalistic pretensions, the latter because He menaced their profits and their comfort. But it is obvious that there was a "Third Force" in Palestine, a pure core of faithful folk who kept true religion alive in an age of disillusionment and worldly materialism, the New Testament representatives of what the Old Testament calls "the Remnant," the "seven thousand who had not bowed the knee to Baal," "God's poor," the faithful in all ages.

Mary and Joseph, and the parents of John the Baptist, belonged to this group; so did the Bethany family; so did the fisher-folk of Galilee, the erstwhile disciples of John; so did the widow in the treasury, who dropped a tiny contribution into the box. . . . They were all there, in the story, quite clear to the reader. The Scrolls seemed to give them life. Among them the old tradition of the wilderness was alive, and this is another feature of the New Testament on which the Scrolls form a commentary. It requires a word of fuller explanation.

The Role of the Wilderness

Deep in the Hebrew consciousness was a distrust of the city. Abraham, with the vision of monotheism in his heart, had left Ur of the Chaldees, the great pagan seaport on the Persian Gulf, because his purpose was to found a nation in the clean and empty wilderness. It was a sound instinct, and the Hebrew consciousness saw the action for the symbolic movement it was. The writer of the epistle to the Hebrews was talking in a familiar style when he pictured Abraham, the father of their race, "dwelling in tents with Isaac and Jacob, the heirs with him of the same promise, for he looked for a city which hath foundations, whose builder and maker is God."

THE WILDERNESS OF JUDAEA *in this panoramic scene is typical of the lonely country east of Bethlehem.*

So, too, in times of national stress, it was the wilderness which suggested itself to the Hebrew mind, and made their rallying cry: "To your tents, O Israel." And during the Feast of Tents every year the city dwellers forswore their comfort and lived on rooftop and in garden in tents, or shelters of palm branches. All through history, too, urban religion, smug and formal and prone to corruption, was never safe from the brusque intrusion of an Amos, or an Elijah, men of the wilds and the empty countryside, swift and ruthless in denunciation of sin, and urgent in calling an errant city multitude back to the simplicities of faith.

It should, therefore, occasion no surprise that, around the time of Christ, a protest movement should have sought the wilderness. Isaiah's writings are prominent among the

Scrolls, and a verse from Isaiah could have been the marching order and directive of the Qumran community. "In the
wilderness," it runs, "prepare the way of Jehovah. In the
desert make straight a pathway for your God."

Nor can it be an accident that these very words find
echo and repetition in the recorded sayings of John the
Baptist. He was "a voice," he said, "crying in the wilderness:
Make straight a pathway for your God." The fervent desert
preacher whose whirlwind ministry forms a prelude to the
Christian story, was obviously under the influence of the
desert religious communities, or perhaps a member of one
of them. His activities were centered a dozen miles from
Qumran. His disciples, who became Christ's "fishers of men,"
were converts who went back to their daily ways of living,
and carried into industrial and urban life the breath of the
wilderness devotion. . . .

The Historians and Qumran

The fact that there was a protest movement in Jewish
religion has always been known. The Essenes were described in the first century. Indeed Pliny, the Roman writer
whose scientific curiosity led him to his death in the erup-
tion of Mount Vesuvius in August. A.D. 79, actually described
a community by the Dead Sea which could easily be the
people of the Scrolls. He had doubtless talked with many
soldiers who had fought through the Jewish War of A.D. 66
to 70, during which the community at Qumran was broken
up, leaving its library in the sheltering caves.

Pliny's account of the Dead Sea contains the following
paragraph. It led to a major archaeological discovery. Here
is the text:

> On its west side (Pliny refers to the Dead Sea), just far
> enough from its shore to avoid its baneful influences, live the
> Essenes. They form a solitary community, and they inspire
> our admiration more than any other community in the whole
> world. They live without women, for they have renounced
> all sex life; they live without money, and without any com-

pany save that of the palm-trees. From day to day their numbers are maintained by the stream of people who seek them
out and join them from far and wide. These people are driven
to adopt the Essenes' way of life through weariness of ordinary life and by reason of the change of fortune. Thus,
through thousands of generations — incredible to relate — this
community in which no-one is ever born continues without
dying; other people's weariness of life is the secret of their
abiding fertility. Below their headquarters was the town of
Engedi, whose fertility and palm-groves formerly made it second only to Jerusalem; but now, like Jerusalem itself, it lies a
heap of ashes. Next comes Masada, a fortress on a rock, itself
also not far from the Dead Sea. And there is the frontier
of Judaea.

THE RUINS OF QUMRAN *viewed southeast from the citadel.
The round structure (center middle) is a pottery kiln.
Beyond are the cemetery ruins.*

It is typical of a too common kind of Victorian scepticism
that Hastings' *Dictionary of the Bible,* in an article of over
eighty years ago, dismissed Pliny's account of an ascetic
community by the Dead Sea as mistaken. With the library
from the caves to point the way, the archaeologists turned
to a ruin at Qumran, and found it to be just such a place as

Pliny described, a sort of monastery without celibacy, as skeletal remains of both men and women reveal, the home of a dedicated fellowship given to discipline, the preservation of the Scriptures, and to holy living. The community was established about 135 B.C. It continued for almost exactly two hundred years. In A.D. 66 came the mad revolt of the Jews against the Romans, over three years of grim and awful warfare, the destruction of Jerusalem, and the systematic ransacking of Palestine for all remnants of Jewish opposition. To the Romans, in the days of the Great Revolt, such folk were partisans, and Vespasian's troops overran and destroyed the buildings. The inhabitants, no doubt, escaped, for they had time to hide their books in the caves. "This treasure we have in earthen vessels," said St. Paul, and he was alluding to a custom observed at Qumran. The books were concealed in great jars of earthenware.

Qumran and Christian Origins

Here then is a vivid if not quite accurate Roman picture of a Jewish community remote from the urban preoccupations and practices of the hierarchy of the Sadducees, and the twin schools of Pharisaism. It was one of many such groups, with associates throughout the land, by no means all of them remote and separated from the tasks of industry and daily living. And it is a fact implicit in the gospels that Christ sought His first followers and disciples among the poor of the land, outside organized religion. Hence, the meaning of the Dead Sea Scrolls for Christians of today. It may be summed up in three exhortations. Let them seek simplicity in their faith, and avoid the perils of social compromise. Let them find unity in a common devotion to their God. Let them be prepared to see the benison of Heaven rest rather on the devoted than the proud, on the humble rather than the great.

But such has ever been the theme and purport of the New Testament, and if Qumran is, in Edmund Wilson's phrase, to rank with Bethlehem and Nazareth as "a cradle of Christianity," it is in this sense that the tendentious words could be true. John translated passive protest and retreat into action, withdrawal and return, if Toynbee's formula may be applied. And since John's converts provided the first Christian disciples and prepared the land for the impact of Christ, Qumran, if John was influenced by the group, may claim a preparatory part.

The Scrolls and Biblical Studies

Textually the Scrolls have provided some enlightenment. (For completeness the theme may stray briefly into Old Testament studies.) They have cleared up a handful of inconsiderable textual corruptions, and thrown light on some minor difficulties of interpretation. Until 1947, for example, the oldest text of Isaiah was dated A.D. 895. A major item among the Scrolls is an Isaiah manuscript a full thousand years older. What has it had to say? Many things. There is, for example, no break between Chapters 39 and 40. How, in the light of this, is the theory first propounded in 1892 by Bernhard Duhm, that there were three Isaiahs, conflated and fused in the first century, to stand? Here is a book, dated at the latest about the end of the second century before Christ, which obviously knows nothing about it. Some individual texts have been notably cleared up. Consider Isaiah 21:28, which, in the King James Version, is quite without meaning. The verse runs: "And he cried, A lion: My Lord, I stand continually upon the watchtower in the daytime. . . ." It should be realized that Hebrew was originally written in consonants only. The vowels were inserted later. Imagine the effects of the system. In English so written "bt" could be, according to the context, but, bet, abet, beat, about, abbot, boat, and so on. "Lion" in Hebrew is built as RH which, properly vowelled, reads "ariah." But "he who saw" is "raah" which, without vowels, was similarly RH. Some early scholar vowel-pointed the word wrongly, and produced "a lion." Read then: "And he who saw cried: My Lord. . . ," Sense is surely restored to a tormented text.

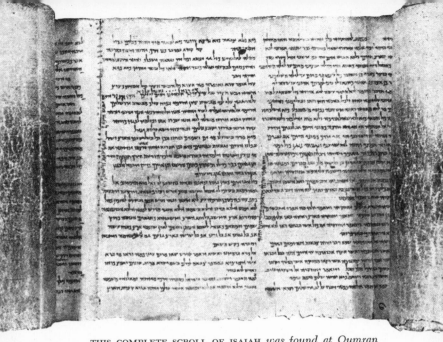

THIS COMPLETE SCROLL OF ISAIAH *was found at Qumran (open to chapter forty in the photo). The scroll consists of seventeen sheets sewn together, measuring twenty-four feet in length.*

There is another mistranslation due to incorrect vocalization in Isaiah 49:12. The older versions speak of "the land of Sinim" which could only refer to China. To the disappointment of those who cherish so far-flung a text, the Scrolls show that the reading should be "Syene," that is Yeb in Upper Egypt. In 20:1, the proper name Tartan, which occasioned some difficulty, reads in the Scroll "turtan" and is correctly rendered in RSV as "commander-in-chief." Add a brief phrase in 53:11 where the Scroll follows the Septuagint rather than the Masoretic text on which our Bibles are based, and you have the sum total. The conclusion is that the Isaiah Scroll, by and large, demonstrates the astonishing accuracy of the text which has been transmitted to us.

It also demonstrates the accuracy of the Septuagint, clearing up in the process a New Testament text. In Acts 7:14, Stephen remarks that Jacob's tribe came to Egypt, "three score and fifteen souls." Genesis, on the other hand, said "three score and ten." It was a contradiction beloved of such as the late Colonel Ingersoll. A Qumran text of Genesis reads Stephen's figure. Hebrew numerals are delicate to write, and Stephen's correct quotation had become corrupted in the later manuscripts behind our version.

Again, what did Christ mean when He blessed "the poor in spirit"? A Qumran text shows that the phrase was used in religious parlance as the opposite of "the hard-hearted." Pity, it may be said, came into the world with Christ. Perhaps the people of the Scrolls had seen a glimmering of that light. With which remark we shall leave them. The story is not yet ended. The archaeologists are at work, and much more may be heard of the true patriots of Palestine, and the stratum of society from which Christ called His first disciples.

Apart from such pieces of notable usefulness, the Scrolls have given little. There are commentaries, one, for example, on Habakkuk, but the exposition is symbolic and mystical, and remote from modern thinking and the plain meaning of the text. There are some biblical romances, embroiderings of the Old Testament story of no more value than the lighter literature of the religious bookshop of today. They have no interest to the New Testament scholar save that they show what may have been the lighter reading in the schools of Judaism in which the first Christians received their education.

ARCHAEOLOGY AND THE
EARLY CHURCH

CHAPTER 11

ARCHAEOLOGY
AND THE EARLY CHURCH

"AND FROM THENCE," CONCLUDES LUKE'S ACCOUNT OF Paul's journey to Rome, "we fetched a compass and came to Rhegium, and after one day the south wind blew, and we came the next day to Puteoli: where we found brethren, and were desired to tarry with them seven days: and so we went towards Rome. And from thence, when the brethren heard of us, they came to meet us as far as the Appii Forum . . . ." (Acts 28:13-15). Over the last miles of the long pilgrimage the Apostle trod the ancient cobblestones of the Appian Way, and moved through a pageant of Roman history. If Paul's spirit was "stirred within him" as he viewed the monuments of Athens, and saw the city "wholly given to idolatry" (Acts 17:16), he must have felt a similar emotion amid the clustering monuments of Rome.

The Prevalent Cynicism of the First Century

The "queen of roads," the Appian Way, runs south from Rome, and along its length stand the crumbling tombs of the proud families who fed on the fat of Rome's dominion.

ALONGSIDE THE APPIAN WAY, *south of Rome, fragments of reliefs and inscriptions of historic value are erected in a brick wall.*

It was a barren joy. The worn Latin on the stone is full of the weariness of the age. *"Misce, bibe, da mihi,"* runs one ("A cocktail, please for you and me"). Another reads: *"Somno aeternali"* ("In eternal sleep"), and shows with the words the symbol of the inverted torch. "What I ate and drank I have with me; what I have left I have lost," runs another. "Wine and lust ruin the constitution, but they make life, farewell."

Some cynicism marks the age, and Matthew Arnold's verse finds a multitude of illustrations. It was somber truth that,

> *On that hard pagan world disgust*
> *And secret loathing fell . . .*

World-weariness was rife. Here is Catullus, poet of high society in the days of Julius Caesar:

> *Suns may rise and set again, but for us eternal night*
> *   remains for sleeping*

"Fruitless words on dust which cannot answer,"[1] he sobs

[1] Catullus, 5:4, 5; 101:10.

over his brother's grave. And here is the stern friend of
Cicero, writing in those days when the Republic was crumbling. The great orator's daughter is dead, and Sulpicius
sends consolation.[2]

Here, he says, is a little thing which may comfort you. On my
way back from Asia I travelled by sea between Aegina and
Megara, and I began to look at the regions round about. Behind was Aegina, Megara was in front. On the right was
Piraeus, and on the left Corinth, towns once in the glory of
their strength, which now lie broken before our eyes. This is
how my thoughts began to run, "Ah! We little men are hurt
if one of ours should die! Yet the wonder is we live so long
when in one place the corpses of so many cities lie." Provinces,
my friend Cicero, are being shaken. Why, in such a day, be so
moved if you have become the poorer by the frail spirit of one
poor girl?

So "the Roman friend of Rome's least mortal mind," as Byron
called Sulpicius.

The cultured Hadrian, who built the mighty wall across
Britain, put the same pessimism into his little poem:

> *Odd little comrade, comfortable guest*
> *Capricious elfin puff of air,*
> *You're off? But where? And when you've left my breast*
> *Tense little traveller, pale and bare,*
> *Will you find anything to laugh at there?*

(trans. Geoffrey Household)

The Optimism of the Early Church

But move on a few generations, and some indication of
the transformation wrought by Christianity is found in a
similar context. Under Rome, deep below the Appian Way,
run the ancient Catacombs. They are cut through the soft
tufa rock, a network of galleries encompassing the city, and
even acting as a cushion against earthquake shocks. In them
are multitudes of Christian graves, and countless inscriptions
breathe the faith of men and women.

---

[2] Cicero, *Fam.* 4:5.

Here lies Ulpia in a small recess. She needed little room, Ulpia, who "sleeps in peace," as the inscription puts it, for she is but a handful of bones, whose fragments perhaps tell how she died. Her friends wrote on the stone that she had not been buried, but "decorated." Hard by, a marble slab records the fact that Eutychia, "happiest of women," lies beneath. A locket with her body depicts Christ bearing the fruit of the tree of life, and above is cut the outline of a strong, sweet face. In strangest paradox the corridors of death contained all that was truly living of ancient Rome. In the simple art and wall inscriptions is the warmth of hope and faith. Pagan Rome above was in the Indian Summer of her imperial strength. Storm was brewing in the vast hinterlands of the twin continents, and all which the Caesars had built and fought for was to pass in ruin. All that had been worth while in Rome's great story was to be preserved for another age by those who bore their martyred dead to burial in the dark tangle of the Catacombs.

The Catacombs — an Art Gallery of Belief

The life of the early Church, the cherished beliefs of its men and women, their favorite stories, their heroism and endurance is read vividly in the *graffiti* and simple art of the Catacombs. Those persecuted generations, vibrantly alive, and unaffected in their devotion, seem in every way more intimately near than those of Medieval Christendom who filled Rome above with churches and somber art.

Withrow remarks[3] on "the complete avoidance of all images of suffering and woe, or of tragic awfulness, such as abound in sacred art above ground . . . There are no symbols of sorrow . . . nothing to cause vindictive feelings even toward the persecutors of the Church; only sweet pastoral scenes, fruits, flowers, palm branches, laurel crowns, lambs, and doves; nothing but what suggests a feeling of joyous innocence as of the world's golden age."

It is a pity that wider areas of these amazing galleries

[3] W. H. Withrow, *The Catacombs of Rome*, p. 227.

are not open to the Christian public. Serious archaeologists have nevertheless done fine work, and some of their findings are a striking contribution to the history of the Church. This is notably true on the vexed question of the strength of the first Christian communities in Rome, for on this subject the Catacombs have a clear and authoritative word to say.

The Lateral Growth of Early Christianity

Consider first the lateral spread of the Church. The adjective is James Orr's, whose striking Morgan Lectures, delivered at Auburn in the State of New York some sixty years ago, first made many Protestants aware of the historical significance of the Roman Catacombs. Orr's lectures, in fact, published in a modest volume under the title *Neglected Factors in the History of the Early Church,* merit, like many others of his apologetic writings, a generous modern edition.

Reliable calculations suggest that the vast tangle of the Catacombs contains up to 600 miles of galleries. The lowest estimate of the graves they contain is 1,750,000; an admissible probability is something like 4,000,000. This is obviously a question which could, with a will to do so, be settled quite conclusively. At any rate some ten generations of Christians are buried in the Catacombs, so that, on the second figure, we have a Christian population, in and about Rome, of 400,000 for one generation. On the smaller computation this would be 175,000.

Such averaging, of course, is not good statistical method, for the number of Christians was smaller in the earlier, and larger in the later generations of the period concerned. But if the figure of 175,000 is taken as representing a middle point in that period, say round about the middle of the third century after Christ, those who remember Gibbon's estimate of the Christian population of Rome will immediately mark a huge discrepancy.

Gibbon's guess, recorded in his *Decline and Fall of the Roman Empire,* was that the Christians at the end of the

third century numbered something like one-twentieth of the population of Rome. That population is reliably estimated at something like one million. The most conservative interpretation of the Catacomb burial figures would, therefore, suggest that not one-twentieth but one-fifth of Rome's people in the middle Empire were Christians, and it is possible that the proportion was at times much greater.

And what of the Roman world at large? The quite impartial archaeological evidence is confined to the capital, but it was a close-knit world, with the Gospel moving through the main centers of population, from the East progressively to the West. Gibbon himself believed that the Christian minority was fairly evenly distributed and that seems likely. If, therefore, what was true of Rome was also true of Carthage and Alexandria and similar main cities, other evidence becomes available. The fiery Tertullian, who speaks for North Africa at the end of the second century, cannot, for example, be lightly dismissed.

It seems impossible to deny the fact that, in spite of State action, the numbers of the Christians were exciting pagan alarm. "The killing beast that cannot kill," of Edwin Muir's moving poem, had done its worst without avail. "Men cry out," says Tertullian, "that the State is besieged; the Christians are in the fields, in the forts, in the islands; they mourn, as for a loss, that every sex, age, condition, and even rank, is going over to this sect"; and, he tells us, "the temple revenues are every day falling off; how few now throw in a contribution." And speaking in brave defiance before the Proconsul Scapula, where exaggeration could only be bad argument, he maintains:[4] "Though our numbers are so great — *constituting all but a majority in every city* (pars paene maior ciuitatis cuiusque) we conduct ourselves in quietness and modesty." He also says that if the Christians in Carthage were to present themselves in a body before the Governor's tribunal, he would have to decimate the city to make an example of them.

---

[4] Tertullian, *Ad Scap*, 2. See James Orr, *op. cit*. Ch. II.

In the context of such claims, made before authorities in a position to deflate mere rhetoric, must be placed the same speaker's celebrated outburst: "We are but of yesterday, and yet we have filled every place belonging to you — the cities, islands, castles, towns, assemblies, your very camps, your tribes, companies, palace, senate, forum — we leave you your temples only."

It is clear that, throughout many generations of the three pagan centuries, the Christian community formed a larger proportion of the whole than the regular church-goers of Britain or America do today. Admittedly the social cleft between Christian and non-Christian was deeper and more pronounced, but the Church could in no sense be looked upon as an unimportant minority. The Christian might have felt the pressure of pagan opprobrium, but he need never have felt alone. From at least A.D. 200 onwards he had reason to regard the future as his, and to rejoice in the growing strength of the Church.

The Vertical Spread of Christianity

The Catacombs also provide illustration of the vertical spread of the faith in society. Viewing the church at Corinth in the middle of the first century, and speaking with some irony of its tendency to a false intellectualism, Saint Paul was constrained to say that their numbers contained "not many wise men after the flesh, not many mighty, not many noble" (I Corinthians 1:26). This remark, which referred to one church only, has been quite illegitimately extended to the whole. It is possible to show from the gospels and the New Testament generally that Christianity from the very earliest times invaded the ranks of the middle and upper classes, and touched the intellectuals. As Orr says: "It may be going too far to say, with Professor Ramsay, that Christianity 'spread at first among the educated'; but this is nearer the truth than the opinion often expressed that Christianity drew the great bulk of its adherents in the earliest times from persons of the lowest and most servile positions

— that, in Gibbon's well-known words, the new sect was 'almost entirely composed of the dregs of populace — of peasants and mechanics, of boys and women, of beggars and slaves.' "[5]

Consider, for example, the case of Pomponia Graecina, wife of Aulus Plautius, who won military fame in Britain. Tacitus reports[6] that this noble lady was tried before a domestic tribunal on a charge of entertaining a "foreign superstition." It was long ago suggested that the lady concerned was a Christian, but failing other evidence the suggestion remained in the realm of conjecture.

That evidence was supplied by De Rossi, most indefatigable of the explorers of the Catacombs. From epigraphical testimony he established the fact that the crypt of Lucina was connected with the aristocratic Pomponian family, one member of which bore the very name of the person mentioned by Tacitus, in its masculine form — Pomponius Graecinus. De Rossi suggests that Lucina (which may be rendered "Lady of Light") was a Christian name assumed by Pomponia Graecina herself at baptism, and that she was the owner or founder of the vault which bears the name.

And if Pomponia was, in fact, a Christian, since she lived on into the principate of Domitian, she may have played a major part in two aristocratic conversions of which there is some evidence — those of Flavius Clemens, the consul, and Domitilla, his wife. The former was the cousin, and the latter the niece of Domitian himself.

It is another pagan historian who provides the clue. Dion Cassius informs us[7] that Flavius and his wife were accused of "atheism," a common allegation against Christians, and of "going astray after the customs of the Jews." Flavius Clemens was put to death, and his wife banished. Eusebius adds his word of testimony, asserting that Flavia Domitilla was exiled for confessing Christ. By an obvious error he calls

[5] *Op. cit.*, p. 96.
[6] *Ann.* 13:32.
[7] 67:44. See Orr, *op. cit.* pp. 117 sqq.

her the niece of the consul. He meant, or should have said, of the Emperor.

De Rossi appears to have established the Christianity of this illustrious pair. He discovered the crypt of Domitilla,

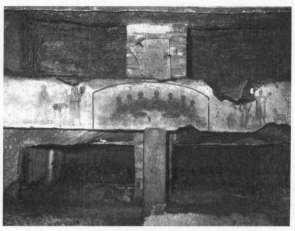

IN THE CATACOMBS *with a view of burial crypts, and a painting.*

and whether the lady was the person of Cassius' notice or her niece, the existence of a Catacomb crypt under the name is sufficient to confirm the Christian connection. Add the discovery of an elegantly constructed "crypt of the Flavians," and Harnack's contention that "an entire branch of the Flavian family embraced Christianity," is established. These facts furnish startling illustration of the extent to which, by the close of the first century, Christianity had pushed its conquests. Next to the Emperor himself, Flavius Clemens and Domitilla held the highest rank in the Empire; their two sons had even been designated by Domitian as his heirs to the purple. It seemed, says Orr, "almost as if, ere the last Apostle had quitted the scene of his labours, Christianity were about to mount the seat of empire!"

It is quite clear that society generally was permeated by

the Christian faith at a very early period of its history. The Church admittedly was neither better nor worse for the social standing of its members. Indeed, in the New Testament documents themselves, Corinth is castigated for its pretentions to philosophy, and Laodicea rebuked for the harmful influence of its wealth. What it is important to point out is that the world of the early Church was such a world as the Church knows today, where people of all ranks felt the attraction of Christianity, and mingled in the exercise of their faith. We have already quoted a letter from a Roman governor to the Emperor in which he describes the grip of Christianity on the province in his charge. He speaks of "all ages, all ranks and both sexes," who had embraced the new faith. It is clear that the world of the early Church was a spiritually hungry world, craving for the consolations of religion, and that the faith from Palestine ran through its stubble like a prairie fire.

The thought which emerges is this — the world in many ways was not very different from the world of today, anxious, war-ridden, disillusioned. Can Christianity do again what it did before? We are, as Professor Butterfield the great Cambridge historian has remarked,[8] in many ways back in the religious situation of the first century, and that situation provides us often with indications of how we should act.

Mithraism — a Rival of Early Christianity

There was a strong rival to the Christian faith in the first centuries of its expansion, and on this theme archaeology has a fascinating chapter to add.

In the autumn of 1954 from the bombed ruins east of Saint Paul's Cathedral in London emerged a little shrine of Mithras, the Persian god of the sun. The existence of this shrine had, indeed, been long suspected, for it is many years since a piece of Mithraic sculpture was found not far away in Bond Court by the Wallbrook. The fragment came from a statuette of the god, and bore the inscription: "Ulpius

[8] H. Butterfield, *Christianity and History*, p. 135.

Silvanus, discharged soldier of the Second Legion, pays his vow."

Ulpius was no doubt up from Monmouth, where the Second Legion was quartered, and visited the shrine of the soldier's god as a modern visitor to London might attend divine service in the Abbey or Saint Paul's. In some nearby shop in the crowded streets of the Roman town, he would buy his votive offering and present it to the deity for life preserved. For Mithras was peculiarly the god of the legionaries, brought from the Middle East by the Syrian legions. It was probably the swelling notes of the hymn to Mithras, sung by thousands of lusty voices as the sun came up, which once chilled the hearts of a Roman army waiting to defend northern Italy.[9] It was a sign that the legions from the East had marched down through the northeastern passes, and were beneath their standards in the camp opposite. That was in A.D. 69, when the Roman occupation of Britain was recent news. When Ulpius Silvanus paid his vow, the religion which had first found acceptance with the garrisons of the Middle East was widely disseminated through the whole Roman Army. Archaeology, and quite notably in Britain, has demonstrated the fact.

The London Mithras shrine is one of a series. There is another on the Welsh border, another lies somewhere under the walls and buildings of York, still awaiting discovery. On Hadrian's Wall, the ruins of which still run from Newcastle to Carlisle, there are two that are known to us. One is in a cave at Borcovicium. This Roman camp sits on the crags twenty miles from Hexham, near the little village of Wall-on-Tyne. Everyone has seen pictures of the wall running in long, firm sweeps over the cliff-tops in this area. It is the best preserved portion of Hadrian's great engineering work, and it is here, on a southward-sloping hillside, that Borcovicium still shows its streets and walls, the foundations of its granaries, and the worn cobblestones which speak

---

[9] Tacitus, *Hist. III*. 24.

eloquently of the Roman's four centuries of sojourn in the British Isles.

On the slope below the camp is the cave which housed the Mithras chapel of the garrison. There is little left to indicate that the legionaries once worshiped here, but one inscription has come to light which reveals the depth to which the cult touched the soldiers' emotions. It reads: "To the best and greatest god Mithras, the Unconquerable, Lord of the Ages, Publius Proculinus, a centurion, dedicates this, for himself and his son, in discharge of a vow willingly and rightly made."

It is the second of the two shrines on the Roman Wall which is of greater interest. Indeed its discovery was quite as striking as that of the London shrine. The shrine is at Carrawburgh, and came to light accidentally. The season of 1949 was quite remarkably dry, and with the shrinking of a peat bog the outlines of a little place of worship came to light, which was immediately recognized as a Mithraeum.

THE GREAT WALL ACROSS BRITAIN *was built by Hadrian, who destroyed Jerusalem in the final Jewish revolt of* A.D. *132. Romans occupied forts along the wall for two and a half centuries, longer than the entire history of the United States.*

Realizing that winter would again flood the ruins, the late Professor Ian Richmond, the discoverer, made hasty arrangements for a competent team to examine it. The work was a triumph of modern archaeological research, for the shrine was, after all, not built of brick or stone. It was a modest structure of lath and plaster, and fragile remains of the sort are uncommonly difficult to interpret and explain. The archaeologists nevertheless succeeded. They were able to demonstrate the periodic destruction and restoration of the temple, according as Mithraism or Christianity won the ascendancy among the commanding officers of the local garrison. They were able to show that the building was finally destroyed in the time of Constantine, when the Empire became officially Christian. The archaeologists' uncanny sleuthing was able to show that the floor of the aisle was strewn with heather, that pine cones were used to make an aromatic altar-fuel, and that chickens and geese were eaten in the ritual feasts associated with the cult.

Kipling's picture was true. He imagines a Roman soldier standing sentinel on some high watchtower of the wall, that wall which so caught the poet's imagination. North lie the gray, dreary moors, as they lie below Borcovicium still, with their steely tarns forbidding in the heather. All manner of evil seemed to lurk in the northern wastes which Rome never surely conquered, and the soldier's heart has fed full, in the night watches, of those ancient fears which have ever stirred in men who grasp their weapons and peer out into the night. The sun springs up, and the legionary lifts his spear in salutation as the trumpets ring out from guard post to guard post:

Mithras, God of the Morning, our trumpets waken the Wall,
Rome is above the nations, but thou art over all.
Now as the names are answered, and the guards are marched away,
Mithras, also a soldier, give us strength for the day.

In the early Persian religion, where his figure first appears, Mithras, like the Roman Jupiter, was associated with light. He is one of the powers of good, who struggled against the forces of darkness and evil. It was a natural step to associate him with the sun, especially at its rising. Mithras, the legend said, had sprung miraculously from a rock, and first found worship among the shepherds of the countryside. After his birth, said the myth, the god set out on a series of toilsome adventures like the Greek Heracles. Chief among these was his contest with a mysterious bull, which he captured and sacrificed. Mithraic sculptures always stress this incident, and seem to imply, by the expression on the god's face, that the sacrifice was a hard and painful duty.

A Mithras shrine has been discovered at Dieburg in Germany which is decorated with a series of wall sculptures depicting scenes in Mithras' life. A pair of horses of obscure significance comes first. A second curious picture appears to show the Evil One lying in wait for the hero. The third panel is more clear. It shows the birth of the god from the rock. The doings of the god in panels four and five are again beyond interpretation. The incident of the sacred bull fills six, seven and eight. Panel ten shows Mithras making his alliance with the sun, while eleven and twelve show Mithras ascending the sun's chariot and going to Heaven. A Mithraeum in Rome develops this last theme more fully.

Christianity's Ascendancy Over Mithraism

If Publius Proculinus from Borcovicium, or Ulpius Silvanus from Caerleon, could walk into a modern Christian church on Christmas Day, they would find a few details oddly familiar. They would find some significance in the Communion service. They would find the adoration of the shepherds in hymn and carol something within their experience. The day, December 25th, would be undoubtedly their own. It was, in fact, Mithras' birthday, captured by the Christian Church. Christ was not born in December, for shepherds do not watch their flocks by night, "all seated

THE SOLDIERS' MITHRAEUM *on Hadrian's wall, at Carraw-burg (above), with a closeup view (below) of the votive inscriptions.*

on the ground," in midwinter Palestine. In the fourth century, with Christ's real birthday long since forgotten, the Church placed the Nativity Feast on December 25th to overlay both Mithras and the gay Saturnalia.

There the resemblance ends. To say that the Christian Church borrowed doctrine and ritual widely from Mithraism is quite absurd, and advanced as a theory only by those who, regardless of history and established fact, find satisfaction in such argument. Christianity won the victory over Mithraism for several clear-cut reasons.

First it built up a corpus of written records. These documents, in plain and simple language, contained, as Angus,[10] the authority on the mystery religions, has pointed out convincingly, something none of the rival cults could match, the compelling picture of an historic Christ, much more appealing in His reality than the legendary Mithras with his strange conflicts. They contained, too, a simple and relevant body of doctrine, adapted for preaching, evangelism, and the needs of daily life.

Secondly, Christianity was universal. Mithraism was for men only. Christianity brought a charter of freedom for women, children, slaves and outcasts. It had food for the hungriest hearts.

Thirdly, and this is a point quite strikingly illustrated by the discoveries at Carrawburgh, Christianity staked all on salvation by faith. In Mithraism, the devotee progressed painfully from rank to rank in the seven degrees of initiation by stern ordeals. At Carrawburgh there is a coffin-shaped stone cell beneath the altar large enough for the body of a man. Here those who sought acceptance or advancement with the god endured the ordeal of heat. The fire blazed on the altar, and underneath the human worshiper endured the demons of claustrophobia and scorching pain.

It would be difficult to imagine anything more fundamentally different from the religion of Christ. Mithraism appealed to the soldiers' desire for a leader, it touched their

[10] S. Angus, *The Mystery Religions and Christianity.*

courage, and spirit of endurance, but it was more like a secret society than a faith. It left untouched the vast problem of evil, and failed to satisfy the deepest yearnings of man. Repentance, faith, and brotherly love to all men, were outside its teaching. That is why today the great uplifted cross of Saint Paul's towers above the spot from which Mithras' shrine emerged.

ARCHAEOLOGY AND THE
FATE OF PALESTINE

CHAPTER 12

ARCHAEOLOGY AND
THE FATE OF PALESTINE

We have followed the Church through the century which saw its birth. There remains the fate of those who chose Barabbas, the path of violence, and that ghastly clash with Rome, which destroyed a land and nation. It is not our task here to tell the story of the most awful war of the century, the Great Rebellion of A.D. 66 to 70, and its equally bitter sequel in A.D. 132 to 135. Archaeology, however, can add some striking chapters to the shocking story, and this account of the archaeology of the New Testament may fittingly conclude with three episodes, one of which lies at the edge of the record, two of which are closer to its heart. We shall tell of the Colosseum, Masada, and the Bar-Kochba relics.

The Colosseum

Italy's largest ruin, the Colosseum, is in danger, according to recent surveys, of falling into yet greater decay. The vandals of Renaissance days, who used the building as a quarry, weakened its structure sadly, and much money will be required to restore it. The old pile looks sturdy enough. To penetrate the tunneled arcades, which provided entrance, is to be amazed at the vast size of the blocks of stone of which the lower walls are built. To look down on the dark oval from an incoming plane on a steely winter afternoon is

THE COLOSSEUM OF ROME *was first called the Colosseum in the Middle Ages. The Romans originally named it the Flavian Amphitheater, after the Flavian imperial family.*

to gain a deep impression of its cruel strength. The aircraft sweeps down toward Rome and the Ciampino airfield. There is first the Tiber snaking through the pastel-shaded countryside, yellow with the silt of Tuscany; then, sharply, Rome, more compact than most other major cities, great apartment houses, which were a feature of Rome in ancient times, the semicircle of Saint Peter's majestic forecourt, the tasteless Victor Emmanuel monument, and the tumbled forum . . . And nearby is the great jagged molar of the Colosseum, a surviving symbol of that harsh, forgotten world.

It was called Colosseum in the Middle Ages. The Flavian Amphitheater, the Romans named it, after the Flavian imperial family who raised it on the site of the lake in the gardens of the Golden House, the huge, mad palace which

Nero was building when he came to his grisly end in A.D. 68. The next year, A.D. 69, saw chaos, with four imperial rivals striving for power on the trampled soil of Italy. Vespasian, the candidate of the Syrian legions, engaged at the time in the bitter struggle of the Jewish rebellion, emerged as conqueror. Vespasian came to Rome, leaving his brilliant soldier-son Titus to finish the war in Palestine with the long horror of the siege and destruction of Jerusalem, one of the grimmest pages of all ancient history.

In Rome, with that care for the urban mob which the emperor could not afford to neglect, Vespasian began to build the Colosseum, and formally opened two levels in A.D. 79. Vespasian died in that same year, and in the two

VESPASIAN AND TITUS, HIS SON, *began and completed, respectively, the construction of the Colosseum.*

brief years of his principate, his son Titus, who succeeded him, added a third level and the upper arcade, the familiar circle pierced with windows, which still survives in part. The finished amphitheater must have been an amazing building. Its timbered floor covered a labyrinth of rooms, dens for wild beasts, mechanical elevators, and an elaborate drainage system. An intricate network of exits, entrances, and numbered corridors and stairways, enabled a marshaled multitude to pass in and out with speed, smoothness, and precision. Forty thousand spectators were accommodated.

But consider the dates. Jerusalem fell in A.D. 70 and in blood and fire the wild revolt was quenched. Jewish prisoners flooded into Rome. They may be observed still, carved on the triumphal arch of Titus, marching behind the conqueror's chariot, with the seven-branched candlestick, looted from the Temple of Jerusalem, plain to see above their heads. Thousands of despairing Jews must have toiled on the Colosseum, and cemented its cruel pile with their blood.

Masada

But when Titus marched home to his hard-won triumphal celebrations in the capital city of the Empire, he left a blazing pocket of resistance behind him. Jerusalem itself was a pile of calcined stone. The seven-branched golden candlestick was stored now with Rome's loot in the Temple of Peace, there to stay until the Goths carried it off in A.D. 410, and buried it with dead Alaric in the bed of the Busento, diverted for the purpose . . . . But down by the Dead Sea a band of Zealots and Daggermen were under desperate siege on Masada.

Who were they, these spiritual descendants of Barabbas and the terrorists of the Jericho road, the Sicarii or "men of the dagger," and the Zealots, one of whose society, a man named Simon, became a disciple of Christ? Some of the determined garrison may have been Essenes, or members of the Qumran community thirty miles further up the Dead Sea Coast. This may be the meaning of a "Qumran-type" scroll as the excavator, Professor Yigael Yadin, describes it, which came to light during the 1966 excavation of Masada. The Roman patrols of Vespasian overran and obliterated Qumran, as we have seen, in A.D. 68. If some of their community retired to join the remnant on Masada, there may

THE ARCH OF TITUS (*above*) *records the destruction of Jerusalem in a relief* (*below*) *depicting Roman soldiers carrying away treasures from the Temple, including the seven-branched lampstand.*

perhaps be substance in the Roman belief that the Qumran complex was a potential stronghold of guerrilla resistance. It is inevitable that the ascetic community would have given shelter to fugitive resistance fighters. Peaceful though it may itself have been, the community could have been taken over by more desperate fighters. And, as we have seen, some of the Qumran writings are not without a coloring of armed revolt.

Professor Yadin spent three years of scientific archaeological investigation and reconstruction on Masada. He uncovered Herod's two palaces on the level summit of the great crag, the Roman camps, and the whole plan of the mighty siege and assault. The results have appeared, superbly illustrated, in Yadin's great book, published in 1967. They confirm the story told at laborious length by the historian Josephus. This sly and clever man had been guerrilla commander in Galilee at the outbreak of the revolt, and had been defeated and captured. By a shrewd playing of his cards he had won, not only freedom, but a post as secretary in the immediate entourage of Vespasian. He used his leisure to write the story of his people.

Herod's Fortress

The stronghold of Masada was one of three mighty forts, built in the rugged eastern hills of Judaea by the first Herod, who ruled the Jews as a puppet king of Rome from 40 to 4 B.C. They were Herodion, Machaerus and Masada, and the last-named was fortified in 36 B.C., over a century before Rome ended the great siege. In the almost impregnable place, it is possible to glimpse Herod's fear-haunted soul, and the shadow of the deepening paranoia, which darkened Bethlehem. The fort is mightily built of casemate-wall and battlement. Reservoirs, huge enough to hold fourteen million cubic feet of water, cleverly channeled out for the flash floods which are a feature of the violent climate, were chipped out of the solid core of the rock. One of the royal palaces stood on the projecting southern prom-

ontory of the summit plateau, skilfully built on three different levels, with a sheer drop beneath. Hence the phrase
"the hanging palace," which recurs in Professor Yadin's
account. It was a magnificent piece of architecture and
engineering, a Roman palace, complete with bathhouse and
hypocaust, the very symbol of that pro-Roman policy, allied
with subtle conciliation of the Jews, which the able Herod
family pursued successfully for a whole century. Wine jars,
stamped with the name of C. Sentius Saturninus, consul for
19 B.C., tell the same tale of skillful collaboration. The jars
were marked: "To King Herod of Judaea," the first inscription ever discovered containing Herod's name. The wine
was evidently Augustus' present to the useful Jewish king.
The view across the sinister waters of the Dead Sea was
superb and appropriate. A secret staircase, "the serpent
path" mentioned by Josephus, had helped in the identification of the vast ruins.

This path, says the historian, "is broken off at prominent
precipices of the rock, and returns frequently into itself,
and lengthening again by little and little has much ado to
proceed forward; and he that would walk along it must first
go on one leg and then the other; for on each side is a vast,
deep chasm and precipice, sufficient to quell the courage of
everybody by the terror it infuses into the mind."

Josephus describes, with details of area and length, the
fortifications and architecture of Herod's fortress and its two
royal abodes, after the fashion which makes him so dry
at times to read, but a blessing to archaeologists. He describes too the storehouses of dates and corn laid up for a
siege, all of which, he alleges, in the clear dry air of the
locality, remained edible and fresh for long years in the rock
reservoirs. Remnants have been found in the long store-
rooms. It was a well-stocked and well-armed stronghold
which fell into the possession of the last desperate Jewish
fighters of the Great Rebellion. Ablaze with nationalistic
fervor, the nation only fell back beaten when the ashes of
Jerusalem covered a million dead, and the land had been

combed systematically at appalling cost of toil and blood. Titus, as we have said, went home for his triumph, while a remnant retired to the fortress, which they had seized at the first outbreak of war, and prepared to fight it out. Titus left his general Silva the task of taking the stronghold, without saying too much in Rome about the last valiant band who were still holding out in the Judaean wilderness.

Mass Suicide

The memorials of the Roman siege are clearly visible on the site. The wild Jewish garrison was ringed in by such walls of circumvallation as those which Julius Caesar so often describes in his war commentaries, and the lines of the digging and heaping of the earth are still clear around the base of the escarpment. The two Roman camps may also be seen. Against the cold methodical tactics of Roman engineers and storm troops, the world's valor had always proved vain. Masada followed Carthage, Capua, Alesia and other cities, which had learned by grim experience the firm and unrelenting pressure of a Roman siege. Inevitably the end came. The Roman ramp, heaped and piled with dogged toil against the great cliff, climbed higher and higher. The covered siege engines rolled up its steep slope. The stone ballista balls, catapulted from their armored tops, poured into the fortifications. They are found in piles. At last the battering rams began hammering the final wall. The garrison built another wall of beams behind it. It was fired in their faces. The end had come.

Josephus' story of the storming makes grim reading. Its every incident may be followed in the recent excavations. Eleazar, the captain of the Jews, made two long speeches in which he exhorted his followers to cheat the victors by mass suicide. There is something peculiarly horrible in his assembling of moral and theological argument, and the Jewish historian reports it all at merciless length. The men embraced their wives and children and cut their throats. They set fire to their last possessions in the corners of their

MASADA ROCK *is the elevated fortress where Jewish rebels held out for three years after the fall of Jerusalem. The Roman siege ramp, well-preserved to this day, is clearly visible in the center of the photograph.*

THE ROMAN COIN *(below) was issued to commemorate the Roman victory over Jewish resistance. The coin includes the words, "Judaea Capta."*

rooms. Ten men were chosen by lot to slay the rest. These lay down by the bodies of their families, and the ten executioners went systematically to work. One man was then chosen by lot out of the ten, and he killed his nine companions. The very lots, fragments of pottery bearing the names of the ten, have been found, the letters still legible on the baked clay. The lots were thrown, no doubt, into a helmet, and one was drawn. Left alone in the charnel house, the lone survivor went around the ranks of the dead and made sure with a thrust here and a slash there that none remained with vestige of life, and then, says Josephus, he drove his sword through his own body. It is possible to picture his end. On the steps of Herod's smaller bathhouse there are the remains of three bodies. The excavators moved the rubble with care. Masses of plaques from scale-armor spoke of a soldier's corpse. Nearby was the skeleton of a young woman, her scalp intact in the dry atmosphere. Her dark hair beautifully plaited, looked as if it had been newly braided for the day of death. The plaster of the wall nearby was stained with blood. Delicate lady's sandals were on the steps, and the skeleton of a child. . . . Was this the last man alive, dying finally by his own sword, after killing wife and child?

So fell nearly a thousand Jews. But two women hid five children in remote cellars, and concealed themselves with food and drink. When the Romans staged their final assault, burst in, and paused in wonder and suspicion at the awful solitude, these two survivors came out, and told what had happened. The Romans themselves, says Josephus, "could take no pleasure in the deed."

Palestine lay in such peace as a war of annihilation can give. A Roman garrison appears to have occupied Masada. It had held out incredibly for almost three years after Jerusalem had fallen. "They make a desert and they call it peace," said a bitter British chieftain, in Tacitus' account of Agricola's raid into northern Britain of A.D. 79, and Palestine was desert indeed. It is difficult to imagine how any further resistance could be possible, and in fact, no resistance to Rome's ruthless rule arose in Palestine for over two generations.

The Bar-Kochba Rebellion

What Hadrian did not realize, sixty years after Titus, was that the ruin-pile of Jerusalem was a matter of sentimental, indeed of fierce religious interest, to the remaining Jews of Palestine. Throughout the world they had again been restive, a prey to one of those waves of passionate nationalism to which, as a race, they were prone. In Trajan's principate, seventeen years before, the great Jewish populations of Cyrene, Alexandria and Cyprus had risen against their Greek neighbors and killed them in hundreds of thousands, only to suffer reprisals as fierce and sanguinary.

In Hadrian's day revolt was localized in Palestine. Hadrian had conceived the idea of rebuilding Jerusalem. Its ruin offended his tidy mind and artistic spirit. On the

HADRIAN, ROMAN EMPEROR *sixty years after Titus, underestimated the Jewish capacity for passionate nationalism, and Jerusalem was destroyed under him in* A.D. *132.*

temple site he proposed to build a shrine dedicated to Olympian Zeus. Nothing could be more calculated to inflame the Jews, and it is odd that the most traveled of the Emperors should have been so ill-informed about the depth and power of surviving Jewish sentiment in the devastated land.

With frightening unanimity, Palestine rose. One Bar-Kochba emerged, a "Messiah of the wilderness," the perennial peril of the passionate land. So unexpected was the explosion, so fanatical its leadership, that Bar-Kochba was for a time actually master of the land, and Jewish coins survive marked variously: "Simon Prince of Israel"; "For the Freedom of Jerusalem"; "For the Freedom of Israel."

Again it took the methodical Romans three years of bitter, agonizing guerrilla war to flush the bands of wild Jewish rebels from the tangled hills, ravines and caves, which had once sheltered David. Losses were appalling. Half a million Jews fell, and Judaea was again left a wilderness. So heavy were the Roman's own casualties, that Hadrian, in his report to the Senate announcing the end of the war, omitted the usual introductory formula that it was "well with him and with his army."

A cache of Bar-Kochba's letters and campaign documents have been discovered in a cave by the Dead Sea. It is strange to read his terse orders. The documents are in varied hands so we may not have the guerrilla leader's own handwriting. Adjutants were, no doubt, the scribes. "Whatever Elisha says, do," runs one command. Another orders the arrest of Tahnun Ben Ishmael, and the confiscation of his wheat. Another called for punishment on some who had repaired their homes, in defiance of some scorched earth policy . . . It is all very cold, hard, and infinitely pitiable.

Ten of the letters have been deciphered. They are signed "Simon Bar Koziba," the hero's name before he took the Messianic title "Bar-Kochba," or "Son of a Star." Knowing His race, Christ Himself had given warning against such dangerous claims: "If any man shall say to you, Lo, here is the Messiah, or there, believe them not, for there shall arise false Messiahs who shall show great wonders, so that if it were possible they should deceive the very elect . . . so, if they shall say to you, Behold, he is in the desert, go not forth."

THIS LETTER *written to Joshua ben Galgola, one of Bar Kochba's commanders, alerted him to the approach of Roman troops.*

The words were lost on the brave, doomed Jews of Hadrian's day. Symbolically, indeed, the land had chosen Barabbas a century earlier. Christ's followers, long since noting the warnings, had left the storm centers of Jewish nationalism, and found manifold homes abroad. It is to be supposed, therefore, that few Christians perished in the two rebellions which reddened two separate decades with carnage.

There was another fragile discovery which throws pathetic light on this tragic rebellion. A small bundle of papyrus documents of the sort described, was found, tied with a palm-fibre rope, in a Dead Sea cave. It was packed in a goatskin bag along with some beads, a mirror, and a

comb, a whole toilet set, in fact, with perfume and powder
container. It was the property, perhaps, of the wife of a
patrol leader in their stern wilderness-war. The poor relics
lie in a glass case in the Museum of the Hebrew University
of Jerusalem, looking curiously modern, dead symbols of
frustrated hope, blind courage, and fatal choice.

OLIVE STONES IN A WOODEN BOWL AND A CHILD'S SHOE
*are among many items recovered from the hideout caves
of the Bar Kochba rebellion.*

INDEX